Elites, Masses, and the Struggle for Democracy in Mexico

A Culturalist Approach

Sara Schatz

PRAEGER

Westport, Connecticut
London

Library of Congress Cataloging-in-Publication Data

Schatz, Sara, 1963–
 Elites, masses, and the struggle for democracy in Mexico : a culturalist approach / by
Sara Schatz.
  p. cm.
 Includes bibliographical references and index.
 ISBN 0–275–96666–6 (alk. paper)
 1. Democratization—Mexico. I. Title.
JL1281.S32 2000
320.972—dc21   99–088487

British Library Cataloguing in Publication Data is available.

Library of Congress Catalog Card Number: 99–088487
ISBN: 0–275–96666–6

First published in 2000

Praeger Publishers, 88 Post Road West, Westport, CT 06881
An imprint of Greenwood Publishing Group, Inc.
www.praeger.com

Printed in the United States of America

The paper used in this book complies with the
Permanent Paper Standard issued by the National
Information Standards Organization (Z39.48–1984).

10 9 8 7 6 5 4 3 2 1

Copyright Acknowledgments

The author and publisher gratefully acknowledge use of the following material:

For excerpts from an interview with Sergio Aguayo. Used with permission of Sergio Aguayo.

Parts of Chapter 3 first appeared with references in *The International Journal of the Sociology of Law* (Academic Press). Used with permission.

Chapter 4 is a version of a piece that first appeared in *Studies in Law, Politics and Society* (JAI Press Inc.). Used with permission.

Contents

Preface

This book offers a sociological account of Mexico's "delayed transition to democracy" for the years 1991–97. Throughout, I will insert the study of Mexican democratization into the comparative sociological analysis of transitions to democracy.

Studies of democratization from non-Leninist civilian single-party authoritarian regimes like the Mexican, have received relatively little analytic attention. Many contemporary studies of democratization focus on the breakdown of military regimes in southern Europe and Latin America and on the transition to democracy and capitalism in Eastern Europe. Democratization in non-Leninist civilian single-party authoritarian regimes has received far less attention. This book seeks to fill this gap by examining the sociocultural sources of delay in Mexico's transition to democracy in the 1990s up to the historic 1997 election, in a comparative context.

Mexico's transition to democracy is clearly "delayed" when judged by macrosociological structuralist theories of economic development, given its level of urbanization, education and industrialization. This is compared with levels of development in already democratized nations. I argue that Mexico provides a prime case for theoretical development because its unusual characteristics provide the best opportunities to test, modify, and update the content of current theories regarding the social bases of democratization. To give a full account of Mexico's transition to democracy, I develop a new model of transitions that extends existing theories of the social bases of democratization.

I argue that the Mexican, and other transitions to democracy, from non-Leninist single-party systems in Asia and African, are best explained by a model of delayed transitions to democracy. Specifically, I explain the sociocultural sources of Mexico's transition to democracy in two ways. First, I argue that the Mexican state's

corporate shaping of social interests, cleavages, and forms of political consciousness has had important consequences for the social base of democratization. This
has caused it to differ from the modal patterns of the democratizing experience in
Western Europe. The complex, and politically divided role of the Mexican middle
classes (simultaneously pro-authoritarian but also favoring the right and the left
democratic opposition), delays Mexico's transition to democracy by reducing the
likelihood of a united middle-class anti-authoritarian coalition.

Furthermore, the authoritarian regime's historical policy of licensing of political
opposition parties also delays the transition to democracy by creating the uneven
development of opposition parties. Each opposition party gains a stake in the
electoral system at a different point in time by carving out its own ideological niche
distinctive from the dominant single party. This inhibits united opposition party
action. Because opposition political parties are not strong enough alone to make a
clean sweep of the institutions of the old regime, the transition to democracy is
delayed in Mexico. I also treat other Asian and African cases in a comparative
perspective to show the explanatory power of the main thesis of the book.

Thus, I develop a "delayed transitions to democracy" model based on the
premise that the corporate authoritarian characteristics of late twentieth-century
regimes differ in ways from the Western European experience that influence their
transitions to democracy. Consequently, my account proposes a sociological approach that explains the dynamics and outcomes of transitions in terms of group
processes (social movements, political contests and compromises between elites,
social struggles over political rights). Although the period of the mid-1990s covered
by this book is a significant one for Mexico, its democratization has been a long,
complex, and drawn out process. Therefore, the sociological account in this book
is a *process*-oriented one that assumes that democratization in non-Leninist single-
party regimes can occur for a protracted period of time without a decisive collapse
of the regime.

The writing of this book would have been impossible without the cooperation
of many institutions and individuals. During the time that it took to complete this
project, the research was funded principally by the Andrew W. Mellon Foundation
grant for Latin American Sociology and by a Ford Foundation Research Fellowship.
I would also like to acknowledge the aid of the *Centro de Investigación de Docencia
Económica* (Mexico) for assistance with data collection. I am grateful to all donors
and sponsors, particularly to David López for his consistent material support over
the years.

Many individuals helped in clarifying the concepts and in producing the pages
that follow. Special thanks go to Ivan Szelenyi, Barbara Geddes, and David López
at UCLA for carefully reading and criticizing early drafts of the manuscript. They
helped me to rethink and amend the presentation of key ideas. A number of
colleagues have provided assistance or have suggested corrections and reinterpre-
tations in parts of the text. For these contributions, I am grateful to Peter Evans,
Jeffrey Broadbent, Charles Wood, Peter Ward, Bryan Roberts, Sergio Aguayo,
Héctor Fix-Fierro, Jaime Cárdenas Gracia, Manuel González Oropeza, Tsai Chia-

Hung, and Bernadetta Killian. Parts of Chapter 3 first appeared in *The International Journal of the Sociology of Law* (Academic Press). Chapter 4 is a version of a piece that first appeared in *Studies in Law, Politics and Society* (JAI Press). I also appreciate comments from participants of the panel presentations at the American Sociological Association, various panels hosted by the Andrew Mellon Foundation Conferences for Latin American Sociologists, and the UCLA Latin American Center Panel Discussion on Mexican Elections 2000 including Denise Dresser and David Ayon. Finally, I am indebted to Javier Gutiérrez-Rexach, Byron Schatz, and Frances Schatz for help and encouragement at numerous stages in the research process.

Chapter 1

Delayed Transitions to Democracy: Mexico in Comparative Perspective

Mexico's transition to democracy presents a sociological puzzle. When assessed in relation to the family of sociological structural theories that attribute the rise of democracy to industrial capitalism and dominance by the middle classes, Mexico's transition is quite "delayed." Widespread and deeper democratization should have occurred earlier in Mexico's history. Mexico has experienced political liberalization and then democratization over two decades, but without an unambiguous transition to fully competitive and open electoral politics. By mid-1999 the largest political party—the PRI (Party of the Institutionalized Revolution), historically referred to as the "party-state"—still controlled the presidency, most state governorships, municipalities, and a 46 percent share of the national vote (Dresser 1999). The major independent political opposition parties each controlled a portion of the remaining 46 percent of the national vote with 8 percent captured by the semiopposition parties.

Mexico's transition to democracy is delayed because, historically, the level of democratization of Mexico's political institutions has not corresponded to what is predicted by the higher levels of the country's socioeconomic development (industrialization, levels of education and urbanization). Lipset (1959:73) argued that Mexico was a "borderline" case that posed problems for the classification of nations as democratic or nondemocratic. Indeed, the application of the social prerequisites predictions of economic development (levels of urbanization, education and industrialization) as a source of explanation for levels of democratization in Mexico's thirty states and the federal district yields contradictory outcomes.[1]

Other theorists have also pointed to the distinctive nature of Mexico's transition to democracy. Rueschmeyer, Stevens and Stevens (1992:199) argue that Mexico's democratic record "is clearly below what one would expect on the basis of the country's level of development," and that this requires "special treatment." The pivotal role of the state in shaping the political articulation of civil society; specifically in linking the interests of subordinate classes to the party is theorized as a central explanation for "weakening the capacity of subordinate classes to pressure for effective political and socioeconomic participation and representation in the longer run" in Mexico (Rueschmeyer et al. 1992:201). The PRI has "demonstrated flexibility in responding to the challenges that have emerged with a variety of liberalizing measures which have extended the space for contestation but stopped short of allowing for real democratization, namely the possibility of a replacement of the PRI by an opposition" (Rueschmeyer et al. 1992:204). Accordingly, in Mexico and other developing nations where the authoritarian cooptation of organized labor has occurred despite capitalist development, the authors predict that the democratizing struggle will be conducted the urban educated, well-to-do middle classes (Rueschmeyer et al. 1992:217).

Treatments of Mexico within the voluntarist or choice models of the transition to democracy also refer to the delayed nature of Mexico's transition to democracy. Middlebrook (1986:146–47) suggested in the mid-1980s that organizational factors (the opposition's historical lack of access to significant resources and power, resistance by existing "official" labor and peasant organization, factionalism, and organizational rivalries) inhibited more far reaching democratizing change in Mexico. Knight (1992:144) argues that while "elite settlements" successfully explain Mexico's postrevolutionary political stability, elite settlements say little about the genesis of democracy in Mexico (Knight 1992:144).

Even theorists who viewed similarities between Mexican authoritarianism and Southern Cone bureaucratic authoritarianism in the 1970s (Cotler 1979:281–82), nevertheless suggested that capacity of the PRI to implement and legitimate the system of domination made the Mexican system distinctive. Cotler (1979:273) predicted in the late 1970s that Mexico could move toward "widespread economic and political repression required by [an economic] stabililization policy" as occurred in the bureaucratic-authoritarian nations of the Southern Cone. Accordingly, Cotler (1979:281–82) predicted this would "undermine the support coalition of the state, provoking a cleavage between state and society, with the consequent dismantling of the political apparatus created in the aftermath of the Mexican Revolution."

True, by the mid-1990s, popular mobilization, often based on economic grievances, had increased dramatically after more than a decade of neo-liberal stabilization policies (GEA Político1996; Latin American Data Base 1996); thus suggesting evidence of a new cleavage between state and society. Yet, one of the most striking aspects of the Mexican regime has been its continued level of support, especially electoral support, even in the face of extraordinary economic hardships endured by most Mexicans, especially since 1995 (Kaufman and Zuckerman 1998:369). As compared with the breakdown of Southern Cone military regimes then, it is the comparative longevity of the Mexican authoritarian regime and its delayed transition to democracy that must be explained.

In this book, I argue that Mexico provides a prime case for theoretical development because its unusual characteristics—a delayed transition to democracy—provide the best opportunities to test, modify, and update the content of current theories regarding the social bases of democratization. To give a full account of Mexico's delayed transition to democracy, I develop a new model of transitions that extends existing theories of the social bases of democratization. I argue that the Mexican, and other transitions to democracy from non-Leninist single-party systems are best explained by a model of delayed transitions to democracy.

Specifically, I suggest instead that a "delayed transitions model" is a more adequate explanation of a pattern of cases of gradualist transitions to democracy from non-Leninist single-party systems because the traditional emphasis on transformative industrialism in theories of the social bases of democratization is modeled too closely on the Western European democratizing experience to permit full explanation of the cases. Although my model builds on the insights of structural theories regarding the social bases of anti-authoritarian mobilization, I also incorporate insights from the comparative literature on the different paths of dissolution of various types of authoritarian regimes to explain the structural interest cleavages and forms of political consciousness characteristic of twentieth-century corporate single-party authoritarian regimes. To support the delayed transitions model, I compare Mexico with Taiwan, and Tanzania, countries also characterized by delayed transitions to democracy in the late twentieth century.

This chapter consists of the theoretical elaboration of my model of delayed transitions to democracy. With this end in mind, I begin with a discussion of the comparative context within which delayed transitions to democracy occur.

GENERAL UNIVERSE OF CASES

Mexico's delayed transition exists within an array of transitions to democracy from non-Leninist single-party systems outside the Soviet orbit[2] including Botswana (regime founded 1966), Ivory Coast (1960), Kenya (1963), Malaysia (1957), Mexico (1929), Senegal (1960), Singapore (1965), Taiwan (1949), Tanzania (1964), Tunisia (1957), Zambia (1964), and Zimbabwe (1979) (Geddes 1999).[3] Analysts of transitions to democracy from non-Leninist single-party regimes have begun to suggest that such transitions are distinctive (Crouch 1996; Holm 1988; Pei 1994). Nevertheless, scholars have not yet developed a comparative social theory of the social patterns, structures, and dynamics of these new *social types* of democratization and democracy.

One reason for the lack of theoretical development of this sub-set of cases is because scholars of transition to democracy in the 1970s to the 1990s (Karl 1986; O'Donnell and Schmitter 1986) and in the consolidation of democracy (Gunther et al. 1995, 1996; O'Donnell 1996) draw their analogies, derive their comparisons, and shape their theories of the transition and consolidation of democracy in the third wave of democratization almost exclusively on the basis of the historical experience of the breakdown of military regimes. The most influential early studies of transitions focused largely on well-known cases of the breakdown of military regimes in southern Europe (Spain, Portugal, Greece, and perhaps Turkey) and in Latin America (Uruguay, Argentina, Chile, Brazil, and Venezuela) (Geddes 1999; O'Donnell and Schmitter 1986; Schmitter and Karl 1994:173, note 1). The current debate on the consolidation of democracies is still based largely on the historical experiences of the ex-military regimes (Spain, Portugal, Argentina, Uruguay, Chile, Peru, and Brazil) (Gunther and Higley 1992). Even in the major sociological critiques of the transitions literature, which contend that it accounts inadequately for social class (Neuhouser 1992) and for cultural dynamics (Edles-Desfor 1995), the empirical refutations are based on the democratization experience of ex-military regimes (Venezuela, Spain).

Because of this improvident focus on the breakdown and transition of military regimes and the consolidation of ex-military regimes, nations whose transitions to democracy differ from this pattern in important ways are theorized as exceptions to the dominant model rather than as a new type of transition. For example, Pei (1994:155) argues that Taiwan's transition from a resilient, stable, single-party regime is "exceptional" in relation to transitions from military rule because its political opening was neither triggered by critical elite splits nor defections from the old regime, by socioeconomic crises, by external market shocks, nor by popular demands for socioeconomic reforms. In another example, Botswana's "paternalist democracy" (Holm 1988) should have achieved "consolidation" as a legitimate and institutionalized democracy after thirty-three years of fair and free elections, if one applied the criterion of consolidation used by some scholars (Gunther et al. 1996). Yet the conflicts over consolidation in Botswana's democracy relate to continuing features such as the mutual support system between urban government leaders and their rural subordinates, and the continued electoral dominance of Botswana's single party (Molutsi and Holm 1989:282). This situation bears little relationship to the central conflict in the ex-military regimes: whether political parties and other major groups in the new democracies will remain loyal to nonviolent means of conflict resolution as the only legitimate type of political contestation (Gunther et al. 1996).

One central departing point for an explanation of the social patterns, structures, and dynamics of these new *social types* of democratization and democracy begins from the very particular meaning that elections have in non-Leninist single-party regimes. To help their regimes gain international legitimacy, rulers in such regimes often decide that competition within a limited range of the political spectrum is a desirable alternative to strict hegemonic rule (Linz 1978b:61). Through semicompetitive elections, power is shared, on a small scale, with controlled opposition parties possessing limited resources. Yet when rulers introduce semicompetitiveness into elections, uncertainty and opportunities for gains or for losses to opposition parties become possible. Semicompetitive elections can become a route to democracy, or at least may lead ultimately to the destabilization of authoritarian rule (Linz 1978b:65). Semicompetitive elections in non-Leninist regimes open the door to increasingly competitive elections as a possible route to power for democratizing oppositional forces without a sharp break in the legitimation structure of the old regime. Delayed transitions to democracy rarely occur, then, unless some elements of competition in elections already exist under the authoritarian phase of the regime. For this reason, in all comparative cases of delayed transitions to democracy (Botswana, founded 1966; Ivory Coast, 1960; Kenya, 1963; Malaysia, 1957; Mexico, 1929; Senegal, 1960; Singapore, 1965; Taiwan, 1949; Tanzania, 1964; Tunisia, 1957; Zambia, 1964; Zimbabwe, 1979), on the average, semicompetitive elections involving limited opposition parties are a central regime-structuring feature leading to delayed democratization.

Within the currently existing, non-Leninist single-party systems, free and fair elections have occurred in four nations: in Mexico since 1996, in Taiwan since 1996, in Tanzania since 1995, and in Zambia since 1991 but not in 1994 (Bratton 1998).[4] In the empirical analysis in this book that follows the forthcoming theoretical section, I focus on the Mexican case but also refer to two major non-Leninist single-party systems currently undergoing democratization: Taiwan and Tanzania over the 1990s. Thus, my analysis of voter alignments and oppositional party cleavages of delayed democracy in the Mexican case can be understood comparatively with reference to other cases of delayed transitions to democracy in the 1990s.

The Meaning of "Delay" in Delayed Transitions to Democracy

In this book, I give three primary meanings to the idea of "delay" when explaining delayed transitions to democracy: each of which is comparative in nature. First, Mexico's transition to democracy is delayed when judged by theories of economic development given its level of urbanization, education and industrialization *as compared with* levels of development in already democratized nations (Lipset 1959:73; Rueschmeyer et al. 1992:199). Thus, the first comparative sense in which I mean that such transitions are "delayed" relates to macrosociological structuralist theories of democratization. Second, when examined comparatively, organizational factors in Mexico (the opposition's historical lack of access to significant resources and power, resistance by existing "official" labor and peasant organization, factionalism, and organizational rivalries) (Middlebrook 1986:146–147) and the PRI's organizational capacity to implement and legitimate the system of domination (Cotler 1979:273) explain historically why more far reaching democratizing change has been "inhibited" in Mexico (Middlebrook 1986:146–47). Thus, the second comparative sense in which Mexico's transition to democracy is delayed relates to organizational theories of political control.

Finally, the comparative cases against which many Mexican actors judge the relative degree to which the Mexican political system has democratized are important for understanding of why Mexico's transition to democracy is "delayed." The Spanish transition to democracy is frequently invoked by democratizing actors in Mexico as an ideal-typic transition compared to which the Mexican transition is thought to appear slow or delayed (Meyer 1998b:45; *Excelsior* 1999d:2–3). Because these empirical-historical events (other comparative transitions to democracy) are used as ideal-typic modalities by many Mexican actors when evaluating the relative democratic character of their own political system, the concept of a "delayed transition to democracy" is an analytically useful ideal-type for explaining the pattern of democratization in Mexico and in other non-Leninist single-party systems.

On a final note, none of these three comparative senses of the meaning of "delay" used in this book is necessitarian or teleological because none assumes that democracy is an inevitable or inexorable outcome in Mexico.

DELAYED TRANSITIONS TO DEMOCRACY IN THEORETICAL CONTEXT

The Authoritarian Statist Structuring of Voter Alignments

Theories of the structural factors underlying the democratization are based on the Western European experience—the two great social transformations of national revolution and the industrial revolution produced various social cleavages, which then became linked to four modern political cleavages: center-periphery, church-state, land-industry, and worker-capitalist (Lipset and Rokkan [1967] 1985). In the Western European period of industrialization, universal suffrage and high levels of political mobilization led to the rise of the "class/mass" parties: Politics were structured by parties that largely originated in, and appealed to, one or another social class or religious denomination (Lipset and Rokkan [1967] 1985:134; Luebbert 1991).

In modern authoritarian regimes, however, the central role of the authoritarian state in organizing social classes, especially the middle-classes, as well as in the organization of labor (Rueschmeyer et al. 1992) suggests that the interest situations of either workers or the middle classes should not be predicted to follow the logic of the Western European democratizing experience too closely. In non-Leninist single-party regimes the "land-industry/rural-urban" social cleavage historically did not translate into a political conflict between conservatives (landed interests) and liberals (the rising class of urban industrial entrepreneurs) (Lipset and Rokkan [1967]1985:134; Luebbert 1991). In Mexico, for example, the concentration of large landowners' economic power and social prestige was broken in the wake of the Mexican Revolution under the political control of a populist authoritarian single party (Yates 1981). Because of this path of social development, the "rural-urban/land-industry" social cleavage did not translate into a "working class/capitalist" cleavage during the phase of industrial growth in non-Leninist single-party systems. Thus, we should *not* necessarily predict that the basis of twentieth-century democratic Western European party systems, namely the party divisions and citizens' voting behavior, will strictly reflect the historical development of these four cleavages, especially land-industry and worker-capitalist.

Instead, in Mexico and Latin America during the industrializing phase of development, the "catch-all" party surged to the front as the preeminent form in lieu of the European-type class parties (Dix 1989:27). Broadly speaking, the Latin American "catch-all" party is one that "rejects dogmatic ideology in the interests of pragmatism and rhetorical appeals to 'the people,' 'the nation,' 'progress,' 'development,' that achieves electoral support from a broad spectrum of voters that extends the party's reach well beyond that one of social class or religious denomination, and that develops ties to a variety of interest groups instead of exclusively relying on the organization and mobilizational assets of one (such as labor unions) (Dix 1989:26–27). Specifically, Mexico's "catch-all" PRI party-state reflects a particular quasi-leftist, historical legacy in which the social conflicts of the transition to industrialization were believed to be managed most effectively under a paternalist, authoritarian, corporate regime.

One central consequence of state-led industrial development managed under a paternalist, authoritarian regime is the development of voter alignments and democratizing forms of party organization reflective of authoritarian statism. The authoritarian shaping of middle and lower-class forms of interest organization should be evident in the linkage of voter alignments to political party structures.

Tutelary Democracy, the Actions of Opposition Parties and Protracted Democratization

Elite theorists have begun to study "consolidation," or whether a political system has become democratic (Gunther et al. 1996; Linz 1990; Linz and Stephan 1996; Schmitter and Karl 1994; Shin 1994).[5] The current notion of consolidation model also relies almost exclusively on the empirical experience of the development of competitive elections in ex-military regimes; in such regimes, the return of rule by the military has been a major threat to the continuation of a civilian-led party system with competitive elections (as in Spain in 1936 and 1980–82, Chile, Greece, Uruguay, and Argentina) (Aguero 1995; Linz 1978b). Yet, from the point of view of the analysis of democratization in non-Leninist single-party systems, a central empirical problem arises with current definitions of consolidation: they are compatible with forms of dominant party rule in which a fairly competitive electoral environment exists. In Botswana, as aforementioned, free and fair elections have been held for more than thirty, since the regime was founded in 1966. However, no electoral turnover of parties has occurred at the presidential level (Africa Confidential 1997; Parson 1982:47–55). In Taiwan, by 1995, the reinstatement of the Constitution, the emergence of a competitive party system, and the freeing of civil society from the dominance of the old single-party KMT has not produced electoral turnover at the presidential level. Unless the contention is that Botswana is a thirty-year-old case of an "unconsolidated democracy," we should not predict the rapid collapse of the old single-party in the transition to competitive politics.[6]

Rather, we should predict the old single party will continue to enjoy electoral and popular legitimacy among significant sectors of the electorate. This follows from the historical authoritarian regime policy of semipolitical pluralism checked and controlled by discretionary executive authority. Like military rules, authoritarian executive elites argue that full and open multiparty competition is not appropriate for their societies at the time of their takeover of the state. For example, Tanzanian leader Julius Nyerere argued in 1965 that the rise of single-party rule was necessary because "the challenging task for the nation was economic development and therefore, there was no room for differences" (Nyerere 1974:2).

Yet, unlike most military regimes, authoritarian executive elites legitimate their rule with the holding of semicompetitive elections with the contention that generalized public participation will led to the eventual development of a competitive democracy through elections. This position may reflect, in an authoritarian manner, the fact that the persistence of democratic ideals has been one of the most notable mass features of political cultures, such as Mexico's (Loeza 1985:80). Citizens therefore are encouraged to believe that the semicompetitive elections and limited political pluralism tolerated and controlled by regime elites are manifestations of the regime's actual democratic character. As Loeza observes, Mexican elections have been viewed by regime elites as "instruments to exercise tutelage over (*tutelar*) political change" (1985:76). "Through participation in the ballot box, the Mexican political system has maintained and periodically updated the mass belief in its own perfectibility, as well as the conviction that its institutions are oriented toward democratic change" (80). Scott (1965:330–35, 371) suggested in the 1960s that "the constant repetition of revolutionary slogans regarding national integration and political equality [by regime elites] combined with the careful penetration of the form of democratic elections between different parties has created in Mexican citizens a body of expectations regarding the probability of political participation and the belief that probably some day, their votes will count."

This notion of regime-sponsored "tutelary democracy" explains why scholars persistently find high levels of support for democratic liberties among citizens living under non-Leninist single-party regimes. After the initial steps toward political liberalization were taken in 1977, Booth and Seligson (1993:111) found that Mexican citizens generally expressed strong support for a political system of extensive participation and for inclusive political rights for critics of the regime. Similarly, King (1993:157) argues that in Taiwan, the experience with limited political pluralism and electoral competition at local levels beginning in the 1950s gradually socialized the Taiwanese to democratic norms, values, and attitudes. By 1995, 53 percent of the Taiwanese population was positively or fully committed to democratic consolidation (Shin and Shyu 1997:118). Crouch (1996:241) states that the Malaysian regime's long history of semicompetitive elections with weak opposition parties has encouraged widespread support for party competition and interethnic cooperation because the dominant party could not be assured of winning parliamentary majorities on the basis of electoral support in the Malay community alone.

For democratizing regime critics, the institutionalization of a party system in which licensed or tolerated opposition is allowed to participate in elections creates a distinctive participatory dilemma: whether to accept the legitimacy of the authoritarian system and participate in its elections with the hope of ultimately transforming it, or to

reject it as a mockery of competitive politics and democracy. Some will argue that the recognition of the principle if not the reality of competitive politics, the opportunity to develop some opposition leadership and organization, and the hope of winning at least some contests is preferable to continuing one-party or no-party rule. Others will argue that such a controlled, pseudo-competitive system will deceive the people, reduce the pressures for real democratization, co-opt part of the opposition, and give a false international legitimacy to an authoritarian regime. (Linz 1978b:62)

One central consequence of semi-political pluralism is the emergence of multi-party democracy from a strategy of "tutelary democracy" in which the old single party will continue to enjoy electoral and popular legitimacy among significant sectors of the electorate. The continued widespread viability of the old single party, combined with the citizens' general desire for a democratic government, results in a slow, delayed transition to democracy.

A second important consequence of semi-political pluralism and the licensing of opposition parties in non-Leninist single-party systems is the uneven development of opposition parties; each gaining a stake in electoral system at a different point in time by carving out its own ideological niche distinctive from the dominant single-party. Electoral rules penalizing coalitions also contribute to the consequence that opposition parties tend, on the whole, to try a strategy of continuing to gain electoral advances by competing as distinctive parties in elections with the party of the regime rather than confronting the regime electorally as a united opposition block (Patterson 1999; Peschard 1997). So for example, in Taiwan, no major political alliances have occurred between the two major opposition parties over the nineties against the party of the regime (Chu 1996). In Tanzania's first competitive presidential election in 1995, the registered opposition parties failed to forge a united opposition alliance against the old single-party (Costello 1996:145). In Mexico's transition to democracy in the 1990s, electoral rules, ideological divisions over statist economic policies and leadership disputes have severely limited the number of coalition candidates confronting the PRI (Dominguez and McCann 1995; *El Mundo* 1999).

This contrasts with the popular upsurge of civil and political society in the breakdown of Leninist and military regimes resulting from the generally shorter, more rapid transitions to democracy and (under the military regime) from protracted state repression of politically autonomous civil society organizations (O'Donnell and Schmitter 1986:54–55). Moreover, unlike the case in the Spanish transition from military rule (Edles 1995), the collective fear of the return of military rule is not an analogous issue in delayed transitions to democracy because the military historically has been successfully subordinated to civil authoritarian rule in delayed transitions.

Thus, in non-Leninist single-party systems, democratizing opposition political parties are not strong enough alone to make a clean sweep of the institutions of the old regime, as in the breakdown of military regimes. This point is important because the actors that constitute the opposition parties orient themselves practically toward the idea that they are promoting the emergence of "democracy," as they variously define it, in their nations. Even regime elites come to justify the institutional changes they make in response to domestic and international sources of pressure as causing their political systems to be more "democratic." Nevertheless, democratization in non-Leninist single-party regimes can occur for a protracted period of time without a decisive collapse of the regime.

Institutional Sources of Delayed Transitions to Democracy: The Incremental Separation of Powers and the Gradual Extension of Full Political Citizenship Rights

Democracy is also a multidimensional set of institutional structures whose central dimensions include the separation of powers or, in the European parliamentary systems—judicial review—and the extension of the franchise that make up the structural configuration of the state (Dahl 1989:221).[7] Each of these institutional dimensions should be considered as a continuum, not an all-or-nothing condition (Collins 1998:15).

In ideal-typic terms, the Western European, often Anglo-based, literature on the separation of powers defines it as consisting of the dispersion of power among a number of actors or units involved in collective decision-making, electoral bodies, legislatures, independent judiciaries, even federalism (Aubert 1983; Dicey [1914] 1982). The degree of collegial power can be understood as "arrayed along an abstract continuum, the number of collegial structures, as is its relative power vis a vis central hierarchy" (Collins 1998:18). Where elected authorities are subject to severe constraints, vetoes or exclusion from certain policy domains by other, nonelected actors such as the armed forces, the autonomy of those actors and institutions from centralized control (Valenzuela 1992; Schmitter and Karl 1994) is likely to be low. The extent of the franchise has been treated historically as the proportion of the populace allowed to take part in politics (Therborn 1990). This is because in the nineteenth and early twentieth century Western European experience, it involved the slow extension of the vote to women, nonproperty holders, or non-heads of households, servants, slaves, and laborers (Rokkan 1961; Therborn 1979).

With the "delayed transitions to democracy" model, I also seek to explain the construction of the set of institutional structures whose most important dimensions include the greater separation of powers and the extension of the meaningful franchise that make up the structural configuration of the state. Previous comparative historical literature on democratization has focused on these dimensions in the context of the Western European experience. First, Marshall's (1963) seminal account of the sequence in which citizenship rights were granted in England (civil, political and social) remains the landmark sociological study of the extension of political rights in the literature (Halsey 1984; Lipset 1973; Lockwood 1974; Mann 1987; Turner 1986). In this account, civil rights or the rights necessary for individual freedom (liberty of the person, freedom of speech, thought and faith) emerged *before* the extension of political citizenship rights (the free exercise of the right to vote by the newly enfranchised and/or lower classes and the removal of the effects, in elections, of the unequal distribution of wealth through a reduction in bribery and corruption and the limitation of election expenses) (Marshall 1963:71–72). Both the extension of civil and political rights, in turn, preceded the extension of the social citizenship rights of the twentieth century (rights of a modicum economic welfare and security) (Marshall 1963:72).

Once again, however, I argue that the corporate authoritarian characteristics of late twentieth-century regimes differ in ways from the Western European experience that influence their transitions to democracy. For example, by the late twentieth century, most corporate authoritarian regimes had already extended the universal suffrage to wide sectors of the population (Markoff 1996:144).[8] In such cases, the issue of the extent of the franchise is not *only* about the further widening of it to previously nonincluded social groups, such as rights of political self-determination for ethnic minorities and social struggles over the extension of the suffrage to extra-nationals living abroad. It is also about the free and fair exercise of already existing political rights such as the right to the secret, non-fraudulent vote (Oropeza 1995; O'Donnell 1996:2).

In delayed transitions to democracy from non-Leninist, corporate authoritarian single-party regimes, it is of central importance to connect the free and fair exercise of the secret ballot with the separation of powers because the checking of the legitimacy of electoral outcomes, juridic-electoral institutions, elections, and electoral institutions have historically been subject to centralized executive control. For example, in Mexico, historically the Mexican Supreme Court exercised self-restraint in not ruling on issues of elections, electoral legitimacy, and electoral fraud. This self-restraint in matters of elections has its historical precedent in an 1882 decision by Chief Justice Ignacio Vallarta, who contended that the Court "is incompetent in origin—that it shall not intervene to solve political questions that correspond, by constitutional disposition, to other branches of government" (*Jurisprudencia* 1985:272; Oropeza 1995:13). This self-restraint enabled the Court's other powers to remain functional during long periods of one-party dictatorships, when it was widely feared that the institution would be dissolved altogether by the executive powers (Barragán 1994).

The 1917 Mexican postrevolutionary constitution also failed to subject elections to constitutional control because the Mexican Supreme Court historically has refrained from involvement in reviewing elections; electoral rights did not receive adequate juridical protection (Garrido 1989:420; Oropeza 1995:14). Rather, historically, in electoral matters, the constitution has not stood as the highest authority over the Mexican political system. This authority has been held by the authoritarian president, as leader of the nation and of the nation's dominant political party (Garrido 1989:420).

In legal terms, this highly anomalous situation created the serious legal problem known since Roman times as *Judex non potest esse testis in propria causa* (The judge cannot be a witness in his own case), in which the authority is judge and party at the same time (Oropeza 1995:14).[9] This institutional situation creates a central dilemma within the context of bureaucratized authoritarian regimes in non-Leninist single-party systems: It links democratization firmly with the issue of the greater independence of institutions (independent judiciaries, electoral institutions).

This leads to the second way in which the corporate authoritarian institutional structure of non-Leninist single-party systems shape the transition to democracy in ways that differ importantly from the Western European experience. In the Anglo-American literature, the extension of civil (especially property) rights was closely associated with the separation of powers. Anglo-American sociologies of law recognize the intrinsic linkage between citizenship rights and the institutional role of the Supreme Court as guarantor of these rights (Aubert 1983; Dicey [1914] 1982; Fine 1984; Marsh 1961; Raz 1979). This Anglo-centric historical focus means that the evolution of the rule of law is associated with classic liberalism and with the extension of liberal, property rights (Abel 1988; Fine 1984), and not with the extension of political rights, as in the case of Mexico, Kenya, Tanzania, Taiwan and other cases of democratization in non-Leninist single-party systems (Barkan 1994:57; Cheng 1989:485; Chege 1994:65). Yet, the struggle for autonomous electoral institutions in Mexico, for example, and the attainment of a comparatively autonomous Federal Electoral Council in 1997, has been a central component of the democratizing struggle in Mexico (Schedler 1998). Some analysts even claimed that the autonomy of the Mexican Federal Electoral Council from centralized executive control is the most important political reform of the 1994 to 1999 period (Pinchetti 1999).

Thus, in delayed transitions to democracy, political citizenship rights are only meaningful within the context of electoral institutions whose mission is to try and ensure adequate juridic legal certainty to guarantee the enforcement of suffrage rights by minimizing fraud, bribery, and electoral violence that threaten the legitimacy of electoral outcomes (Rokkan 1961, 1970; Linz and Stephan 1996; Garrido 1989:418). The delayed transitions model attempts to explain these institutional outcomes of democratization (the separation of powers, the increasing autonomy of institutions and the extension of the meaningful franchise) with reference to group processes (social movements, political contests and compromises between elites, social struggles over political rights). This involves an analysis of the struggle for political rights (the franchise and rights to political self-determination, among others), and the greater independence of collegial institutions (independent legislatures, judiciaries, electoral institutions) within the context of bureaucratized authoritarian regimes.

THE "DELAYED TRANSITIONS" MODEL IN FORMAL TERMS

The delayed transitions model provides alternative predictions about the social bases of democratization, the nature of relations between the state and civil society and the sequencing of the extension of what Marshall (1963) refers to as "citizenship rights" (civil, political and social rights) in the transition to democracy from non-Leninist single-party regimes, as compared with elite and structural models (Table 1.1).

The logic of political modernization and class-analytic accounts is that economic development processes cause the mobilization of the anti-authoritarian middle classes (Lipset 1959, [1960] 1981, 1994; Lipset et al. 1993) and/or the democratizing mobilization of a working class, or a working class/middle-class alliance (Rueschmeyer et al. 1992). Economic development processes in delayed transition to democracy can also be predicted to involve the mobilization of anti-authoritarian sectors of the middle classes and/or the working classes as in the Western European experience.

Nevertheless, interests and forms of political organization have been shaped in important ways by the corporate structure of the modern authoritarian regimes. In contrast to transitions to democracy from military regimes, the early onset of semicompetitive elections as a democratic form of regime legitimation in non-Leninist single-party regimes structures a situation in which the political opposition is unable or unwilling to form a united coalition to overturn the old regime in a rapid or decisive manner. This results in the slow, incremental growth of an anti-authoritarian critical stratum, often holding multiple, conflicting value positions.

Therefore, as the result of the historical authoritarian statist structuring of voter alignments and forms of political organization, the delayed transitions model first predicts that the analysis of voter alignments will reveal the anti-authoritarian mobilization of democratizing middle classes and the sectors of the nonpriviledged classes but also predicts no major political alliances or convergence between them. As a corollary, the delayed transitions model predicts that significant sectors of the population will view the single party as legitimate and believe that democracy either already exists or will be created by the single-party regime.

The second prediction of the "delayed transitions model" relates to the social processes by which citizens and elites construct democratic state institutional structures through collective forms of organization (political parties, civic associations, social movements). Given the historical, centralized executive control over elections and the checking of the legitimacy of electoral outcomes in non-Leninist single-party regimes, the delayed transitions model predicts that democratization also involves the continual, ongoing, social struggle over the incremental extension of political rights; and the effort to disperse decision-making power to a wider number of actors not affiliated with the party-state in collective decision-making bodies (electoral bodies, legislatures, independent judiciaries, federalism).

Table 1.1
Predictions by Elite Models, Social Structural Models, and Delayed Transitions to Democracy Model for Democratization

Elite Model
    Elites Compromise

        (1) Elites negotiate political pacts, construct a new constitutional regime based on competitive elections. No one group is able to dominate the democratic process.

        (2) Firstcompetitive election with new political parties demarcates beginning of democratic regime. Consolidation phase moves polity toward presidential–or–parliamentary type political system.

Social Structural Models
    Political Modernization

        (1) Industrialization entails urbanization, rising incomes, rising rates of education, literacy, and increased access to mass media. These social process result in a diminution of support for traditional values and contestation of the old elites' hold on the political machinery, and the in the expansion of political and civil rights through the development of a party system.

        (2) An expanding, highly educated, more economically interdependent urban middle-class is hypothesized to be less tolerant of authoritarian rule and is the premier social actor pressing for expanded political rights.

    Class-Analytic Model
        Conflict between Classes (1) Mobilization of the working class via leftist political parties and unions.

        (2) Working class agitation in favor of expanded suffrage rights.

    Anglo-based Models of (1) Citizenship rights granted sequentially—civil, political, social.
    Citizenship Extension

        (2) Evolution of rule of law centrally associated with classical liberalism and with extension of civil (property) rights.

Delayed Transitions Model
    Authoritarian Corporate
    Structuring of Interests and Forms
    of Political Consciousness (1) Authoritarian Corporate organization of interests inhibits development of independent working class consciousness, creates state-dependent middle-class.

        (2) Demands for political participation stemming from socio-economic development processes mediated through regime-sponsored limited political pluralism.

        (3) Dual but nonpolitical allied mobilization of sectors of anti-authoritarian middle-classes/nonprivileged classes with distinctive interests, political, and economic values.

        (4) Authoritarian corporate control over elections creates continual, ongoing social struggle over extension of political rights linked to the democratizing effort to disperse power in collective decision-making bodies (legislatures, independent judiciaries, electoral bodies, federalism).

        (5) Continued legitimation of old single party into period of competitive elections suggests new type of paternalist democracy.

The Mexican Case of a Delayed Transition to Democracy: Points of Orientation to the Book

The chapters that follow involve above all a *sociological* study of historical change. This means that the presentation is not a strictly chronological or narrative history, but rather a selected series of analytic interpretations of democratization framed in categories and frameworks appropriate to the explanation of general sociological process of delayed transitions to democracy.

As indicated, I explain delayed transition to democracy by reference to structural processes (class, cultural beliefs, economic and political interests) occurring in the larger society. In addition, I give equal attention to major institutional dimensions of democratization (the separation of powers and the extension of the meaningful franchise) as outcomes to be explained. The analysis of the "process" oriented (formally rational) and "content" oriented (substantively rational) motives of actors in social movements, and the analysis of political contests and compromises between elites show how social actors in groups converge and diverge in their democratizing strategies toward the construction of a democratic political order.

Part of the analysis, then, is an attempt to explain the institutional outcomes of delayed democratization by referring to the group processes (social movements, political contests, and compromises between elites) occurring in the larger society that provided the mechanisms that link external structural changes in society to institutional changes.[10] By combining structural and group-process analyses, I try to join the macroscopic and microscopic levels of social analyses (Alexander et al., 1987).

This emphasis on social structure and institutions means giving less attention to many other topics that interest political scientists, political historians, and linguistically oriented cultural sociologists. The topics "left out" of the analysis include the in-depth study of elite strategies and behavior within the PRI; cultural analyses of collective democratic discourses of civil society; and the detailed history of opposition parties.

From a theoretical point of view, this study is a comparative one. While the analysis focuses closely on the Mexican case, I also identify the combinations of the determinants explaining democratization from other single-party regimes including Taiwan and Tanzania.

The Organization of the Book

Chapter 2 begins with the twentieth-century historical context of Mexico's corporate concentration of power and the use of meta-constitutional modes of power that have shaped the pathways of Mexico's transition to democracy. In a large-scale empirical analysis, I demonstrate how the development of the corporate social organization of interests and the historical subordination elections and electoral legitimation to presidential control have shaped party emergence, sociopolitical interest cleavages, forms of political consciousness and state-civil society relations in Mexico's democratization over the 1990s. This chapter shows how interest cleavages and forms of political consciousness in Mexico's delayed transition to democracy do not always follow the expected rational choice, objective interest cleavages, political party formations of state-civil society relations of the European democratizing experience and the various theories of the European experience referred to by the major sociological structural theories of the sociocultural bases of democratization (Lipset 1959, 1994; Lipset et al. 1993; Inkeles 1991; Diamond 1992; Bollen 1979; Moore 1966; Therborn 1979; Rueschmeyer et al. 1992).

Chapter 3 analyzes the rise of judicial review, a central aspect of the separation of powers. Current theories of the breakdown of authoritarian rule generally do not mention the role of supreme courts in the democratization process (O'Donnell and Schmitter 1986; Diamond et al. 1989; Gunther and Higley 1992), despite the important fact that in the transition from authoritarian rule, it must be turned into a defender of the democratic order endowed with legitimate powers of compulsion if the separation of powers is to be guaranteed (Bailey and Valenzuela 1997; Oropeza 1995; Lipjart and Waisman 1996).

In chapter 3, I analyze the 1994 judicial reforms in Mexico as an exemplar of movement on the continuum toward the greater separation of powers. These reforms resulted in an increase in the Mexican Supreme Court's powers of judicial review of legislation in the post-1994 period. My central hypothesis is that the Supreme Court's promulgation and exercise of expanded abstract powers of judicial review of legislation is used both by reformist authoritarian politicians and by democratizing groups, respectively, (1) to increase the perception of democratic legitimacy for an authoritarian regime in crisis, and (2) as an anti-authoritarian strategy in the effort to effect the legal leveling of authoritarian political elites to the rule of law (Weber 1978:813).

In my empirical analysis I demonstrate the shift from a Mexican Supreme Court with no generalizable powers of judicial review (before December 1994) to a Mexican Supreme Court with the power to generalize the effects of its powers of judicial review (after December 1994). I contend that the events of these initial years are sufficient to show a trend toward formal rationalization and to demonstrate the tension-ridden nature of this process. Indeed, I argue that the earliest years of Supreme Court's shift to generalizable powers of the judicial review of legislation show most clearly the strongest struggles over the scope and reach of its new powers.

Delay in the movement toward the greater separation of powers in the Mexican transition to democracy is explained, in part, as the result of the fact that the punitive consequences of legal formalism are not actually implemented in many cases. This is because decisions resulting from the application of principles of abstract formal justice can be damaging to the interests of actors of the old regime accustomed to extralegal, informal justice.

In chapter 4, I treat the Mexican social struggle to extend the meaningful franchise. The franchise is meaningful only within the context of institutions (the separation of powers) designed to ensure that the structure of power within which participation occurs ensures that the vote is exercised in a nonfraudulent manner. Current theories of the original extension of franchise and other political citizenship rights in democratizing contexts are quite Anglo-American-centric in focus (Marshall 1963; Mann 1987; Aubert 1983; Dicey [1914] 1982; Fine 1984; Marsh 1961; Raz 1979). This Anglo-American focus of the comparative historical accounts of the extension of franchise rights must be modified in order to account for how the historical fusion of party and state in Mexico has impeded the free exercise of already existing political rights and delays the extension of political rights to a greater proportion of the populace.

Specifically, in chapter 4, I show how the intrinsic institutional party-state connection shapes multiple dimensions of the broader social struggle for political citizenship rights: (1) through the effort of civic groups to sever party-state connection in the administrative justice of electoral law (Aguayo 1995); (2) through the efforts of reformist authoritarian elites to extend the secret ballot within the dominant party (PRI) itself (*PRI: Consulta* 1999); (3) through the effort of intellectuals and oppositional party members to extend the secret ballot to Mexican citizens abroad (Ross Pineda 1999); and (4) through the effort of indigenous groups to redefine the juridic framework with the Mexican State based on radical democratic claims (EZLN *Reformas* 1996).

I argue that delay in the Mexican transition to democracy is, in part, the result of the fact the further extension of franchise rights to Mexican nationals abroad and the jurifidication of political rights to self-government for indigenous groups are perceived as damaging to the electoral interests of the old regime and as threatening to the territorial integrity of the nation. I conclude that Mexico's delayed transition to democracy provides an important case outside of the orbit of the Anglo-centric narrative of the extension of political rights. The dualistic struggle to extend new political rights and to ensure the effective exercise of existing political rights is a comparative feature of other bureaucratized late twentieth-century authoritarian states undergoing democratization (Taiwan, Malaysia, Tunisia, Zambia, Tanzania, Zimbabwe, Kenya, and Singapore, among others).

In chapter 5, I identify the combinations of the determinants explaining democratization from other single-party regimes including Taiwan and Tanzania. This provides the book greater generalizability to the family of cases that constitute delayed transitions to democracy.

NOTES

1. Current measurements used to assess how closely a nation approximates an ideal-typic "liberal democracy" are usually cross-national in nature; not intranational, that is, they measure differing degree of civil and political liberties; gross rates of GNP or GDP, education or literacy across nations (Bollen 1980). This means then, that to test or specify the social requisites theory across states *within* a nation, we must turn to Lipset's (1959) original indices. The social requisites theory predicts the following for stable democracies: (1)

Measures of industrialization in which the percentage of the labor force in agriculture per state had already dropped to below 20 percent; (2) measures of urbanization in which over 43 percent live in cities larger than 20,000; 87 percent live in cities over the size of 100,000 and 38 percent of the population reside in a Metropolitan area (over 1 million), and (3) measures of education (96 percent literacy) (Lipset 1959:76–77). By the strict criterion of European stable democracies, the ecological data give us contradictory predictions about how the spread of democracy should occur in Mexico. For example, measures of industrialization predict that over half of all Mexican states should have already become democracy in 1990 because by then the percentage of the labor force in agriculture per state had already dropped to below 20 percent (INEGI 1990). Yet, measures of urbanization suggest that either virtually all Mexican states should already possess a democratic form of government since over 43 percent live in cities larger than 20,000; and 87 percent live in cities over the size of 100,000. On the other hand, measures of the metropolitan population predict that none of Mexico's thirty-one states, except the Federal District, should be democratic because in no state does 38 percent of the population reside in a Metropolitan area (over 1 million) (Lipset 1959:76–77). Similarly, ecological measures of education predict only Mexico City and the federal district have a sufficiently literate population to warrant democracy (96 percent literacy—fourteen states did met the literacy criterion of over 90 percent in 1990). So, this theory predicts none, half or all of Mexico's states possesses the social prerequisites for a democracy, that is, it is a theory that gives us contradictory propositions.

In fact, Lipset himself argued that a distinctive pattern for countries such as Ghana, Tunisia or Mexico, which "avoid Communist or military dictatorship political developments" existed in which "an educated minority uses a mass movement expressing leftist slogans to exercise effective control, and holds elections as a gesture toward public opinion, and as a means of estimating public opinion, not as effective instruments for legitimate turnover in office of governing parties" (1959:101). In such nations, he argued that an open party system representing "basically different class positions and values" was unlikely (Lipset 1959:102).

2. See Jowitt (1974) for an analysis of the characteristics that define the Leninist regimes.

3. Geddes (1999) defines the entire universe of single-party regimes to include three pure categories and three hybrid categories: (1) non-Communist single parties: Bolivia (1952–64); Botswana (1966–); Cameroon (1961–83); Ivory Coast (1960–); Ethiopia (1991–); Guinea (1958–84); Guinea-Bissau (1974–80); Kenya (1963–); Madagascar (1960–12); Malaysia (1957–); Mali (1960–68); Mexico (1929–); Nigeria (1960–74); Rwanda (1962–73, ethnic); Senegal (1960–); Sierra Leone (1968–92); Singapore (1965–); Taiwan (1949–); Tanzania (1964–); Turkey (1923–46); Zambia (1964–91); and Zimbabwe (1979–); (2) single parties (Communist, not externally imposed): Albania (1946–91); Angola (1976–); Cambodia, Pol Pot (1975–79, 1997–); China (1949–); Laos (1975–); Mozambique (1975–); Nicaragua (1979–90); Soviet Union (1917–91); North Vietnam (1954–); South Yemen (1967–90); and Yugoslavia (1945–89); (3) single parties (externally installed and/or maintained): Afghanistan (1979–93); Bulgaria (1947–90); Cambodia (1979–90); Czechoslovakia (1948–90); East Germany (1945–90); Hungary (1949–90); and Poland (1947–89). The three hybrid categories include (4) single-party/military/personal: Egypt (1952–); Indonesia, Suharto (1967–); Malaysia (1962–88); Paraguay (1957–93); and Syria (1963–); (6) single-party/military: Algeria (1963–92); Burundi (1966–87, ethnic); Congo (1968–92); and Rwanda (1973–94); and (7) personality/single-party: Bangladesh (1971–75); Congo (1963–68); Cuba (1959–); Ga-

bon (1960–); Ghana (1960–66); Honduras (1932–56); Panama (1968–81); Romania (1945–90); and Rwanda (1973–94).

4. In cases such as in Kenya, Zimbabwe, and the Ivory Coast, where limited political pluralism and semicompetitive elections are controlled by regime elites even more tightly than in Mexico, Taiwan, and Tanzania, single-party regimes have tried to "negotiate institutional changes that will allow the opposition some participation and satisfy international donors and lenders, while not actually giving up control of the government and the resources attached to it" (Geddes 1999:19).

5. Elite scholars define "consolidation" as occurring "when a regime allows for the free formulation of political preferences, through the use of basic freedoms of association, information and communication, for the purpose of free competition between leaders to validate at regular intervals by nonviolent means their claim to rule . . . without excluding any effective political office from that competition or prohibiting any members of the political community from expressing their preference" (Linz 1975:182–183). A corollary criterion used for defining consolidation is "the absence of a politically significant anti-system party or social movement" (Gunther et al. 1996:153). After thirty years of elections under free and fair conditions, the Botswana regime does resemble a parliamentary democracy in which the National Assembly functions along the lines of the Westminster model. Instead, the Botswana parliament is like the traditional African *kgotla* (assembly): It functions "to audit proposals made by those in authority, to approve them and occasionally reject them" (Colclough and McCarthy 1980:46). In Taiwan, by 1995, the reinstatement of the Constitution, the emergence of a competitive party system, and the freeing of civil society from the dominance of the old single-party KMT created a new type of democratic system, neither parliamentary nor completely semipresidential (Chu 1996). Neither the president nor the premier has the power to dissolve the Legislature Yuan, but neither can the Legislature Yuan unseat a cabinet with a normal vote-of-no-confidence procedure. This system has created an institutional mechanism that requires unusually high levels of compromise among political forces if the government is to function (Chia-Ling 1998).

6. According to O'Donnell (1996:37), the concept that a polyarchy has been in a state of "protracted consolidation" for some twenty (or more) years suggests "that there is something extremely odd about this type of thinking."

7. Robert Dahl's (1989:221) well accepted definition of a "polyarchy" with its seven attributes: (1) elected officials, (2) free and fair elections, (3) inclusive suffrage, (4) the right to run for office, (5) freedom of expression, (6) alternative information, and (7) associational autonomy is subsumed in my definition.

8. The countries not claiming to have universal suffrage in 1994 included Guinea, Burkina Faso, Sudan, Swaziland, United Arab Emirates, Lebanon, Saudi Arabia, Moan, Quatar, Kuwait, Bahrain, Afghanistan, Bhutan, Brunei, Fiji, and Tonga (Markoff 1996:144).

9. Historically, the Mexican president delegates this responsibility to his interior minister and to the collegial administration of electoral justice embodied in the IFE (Federal Electoral Institute) and the TRIFE (its juridical wing-Regulatory Tribunal of the Federal Electoral Institute). The president, the interior minister, and the administrative apparatus, not the Supreme Court, are formally the ultimate authorities over the validity of elections. Despite various electoral reforms, elections, electoral law, and the checking of political legitimation have not been subject to constitutional review during the twentieth century (Oropeza 1995).

10. The dichotomy between process-oriented and content-oriented strategies shows how the individual participates in democratizing social processes and social change in a synthetic manner that accommodates both instrumental and affective dimensions. The instrumental

mode refers to the disciplined organization of activities toward the accomplishment of designated tasks; the affective mode refers to expressive, gratificatory or value-originated attachments to both human and nonhuman objects (Smelser 1999). For example, process-oriented strategies or formally rational conduct refers to the increasing emphasis on conduct guided by calculation, instrumentalism, labor, and self-control and corresponds to instrumental modes of behavioral orientation (Feldman 1991; Schluchter 1981). Content-oriented or substantively rational conduct, on the other hand, is expressed by conduct guided by norms or personal loyalty, religious and/or value-rational orientations (Brubaker 1984; Kronman 1983:72–95; Levine 1985:150–162). Formal (instrumental) and substantive (affective, value-rational, religious) dimensions of conduct are intimately interrelated and indeed opposed in an "insoluble conflict" (Weber 1978:657).

These two modes of human action are reflected in the distinction between interests and ideology: the pursuit of economic gain is one variety of instrumental activity, and beliefs in the legitimacy of the mandate of political rulers to rule can be regarded as one organization of affective attachments. Both interest-based and normative conduct identify aspects of human action but not discrete orientations because "in fact the two orientations are often so inextricably meshed that it becomes difficult to distinguish between them" (Smelser 1999:93). My dual methodological focus throughout the book on both interests and beliefs also avoids a reductionistic theory or one that posits a sole explanatory variable such as "interest" for a variety of phenomenon that explain democratization (Stinchcombe 1978). Interestingly, Weber's use of the concepts of formal and substantive rationality in his empirical analysis of democratization was also of a case of democratization (the German case) frequently considered to be "delayed," especially when implicitly contrasted with the Anglo-American cases (Collins 1998:16; Eliason 1998:51).

Chapter 2

Sociocultural Sources of Delay in Mexico's Transition to Democracy: Voter Alignments and State-Civil Society Relations (1991–97)

In this chapter, I analyze the sociocultural bases of Mexico's delayed transition to democracy.

Toward this end, I make three interrelated arguments in this chapter. First, I begin with a historical overview of the unique features of Mexico's presidentialist regime and the historical elite struggle over constitutionalism and the development of Mexico's specific form of authoritarianism. This brief historical overview is important to contextualize the second aspect of my argument: to demonstrate historiographically how the corporate authoritarian structure of Mexico's authoritarian regime has shaped both interest articulation and forms of democratizing party organization. Third, in a large scale empirical examination of over thirty-four thousand voters using logit regression analysis and in the examination of the attitudes among self-declared supporters of Mexico's three principal political parties, I demonstrate empirically that one central consequence of state-led industrial development managed under a paternalist authoritarian regime is the development of voter alignments and democratizing forms of party organization and values reflective of authoritarian statism.

OVERVIEW

In the post-1994 period, several interrelated transformations of Mexican society, and its political and legal institutions were taking place that accelerated changes begun as early as 1977. These changes included: (1) efforts to expand the Mexican Supreme Court's powers of judicial review and to increase the autonomy of Mexico's electoral institutions from centralized control, (2) the sharp increase in the organization and intensity of citizen protests and social movements demanding the extension of political citizenship rights, (3) the struggle of indigenous insurgents for political rights to self-government, (4) an increasingly critical and freer media, (5) increasingly assertive and electorally successful political opposition parties, and (6) the attempt to transform the Chamber of Deputies from a party-state controlled body into an opposition controlled one.[1] In response to these sociopolitical changes, scholars, politicians, reporters, and citizens began to classify the post-1994 acceleration of Mexico's 21 years of democratization as the "long" (Meyer 1998), the "gradual" (Aguayo 1998b), the "veiled" (Schedler 1998), and the "detained" (Gomez 1999) transition to democracy. Some analysts even claimed that these transformations had altered the entire framework of the Mexican political system by the time of the 1997 election (Hellman 1997:92; Bailey and Valenzuela 1997:43).

Sociologically, the dilemma for democratizing elites in paternalist authoritarian regimes such as the Mexican is either to follow strategies aimed at changing the political system entirely or to merely effect a shift in the rulers through semicompetitive elections. In Mexico since the late seventies, most democratizing elites have opted for the latter as the Mexican left has slowly shed its revolutionary approach to social change in favor of incorporation into political parties and the electoral struggle (Woldenburg 1997). The masses, however, are far less skeptical of their rulers in terms of its basic political legitimation. More than half of those Mexican citizens surveyed in the Federal District in 1991 already believed that Mexico already had a democratic system of governance in place as defined in terms of alternation of political parties in power (CIDE 1991). In 1991, a majority of academics classified the Mexican political system as "authoritarian" (Cornelius et al., 1989:8). In 1997, another poll showed that a majority of middle-class Mexican citizens in major metropolitan cities believed, as in the 1991 poll, that the Mexican political system was already a democratic one (Meyer 1998; Aguayo 1999; Rivapalacio 1998). This strongly suggests conflicting interpretations between democratizing elites and mass social actors over basic definitional properties of democracy and democratization. It also speaks to the continuing capacity of rulers to successfully convince the majority of its citizens of its paternalist concern for their social welfare and its commitment to democracy and democratization in the early 1990s.

THE RISE OF MEXICO'S PRESIDENTIAL REGIME IN HISTORICAL PERSPECTIVE

Mexico's presidentialist regime has historically been characterized by certain structural features resulting from its revolutionary consolidation that led to the development of a hypercentralized, authoritarian presidentialism also known as "meta-constitutionalism." This refers to a process in which rules, policies and institutions were subject to informal negotiations (Garrido 1989; Bailey and Valenzuela 1997:44; Rueschmeyer et al. 1992:199; Weinert 1977:xii–xiii; Reyna 1977:160–61; Cornelius 1986:117–20; Levy 1989). Viewed historically, the origins of the Mexican regime has its roots in the nineteenth-century vacillation of Mexican elites between two ideal-typic regime strategies—despotic absolutism and constitutionalism—(Huerta 1993). In this elite struggle, the forces of despotism dominated over the forces of constitutionalism despite brief periods of formal constitutional rule (1824–30; 1867–76) (Meyer et al. 1994; Camp 1993).[2]

The failure of the constitutionalist project in the nineteenth century meant that the Mexican regime did not consolidate its incipient development toward the rule of law. Individual rights over life, property, freedom of speech, assembly, and press were extended but political rights were strongly curtailed.[3] The rule of law as protected by an independent judiciary based on Anglo-American notions of the separation of powers similarly was subordinated in the nineteenth century to the centralizing project of the state, which evolved in an increasingly despotic direction.[4] Furthermore, the inability of the dominant classes to institutionalize contestation (elite turnover) among themselves also precluded the resolution of the absolutist/constitutionalist struggle until after World War II, as in the French, Spanish, and Italian cases (Mann 1987).

Constitutionalists again tried to consolidate power after winning the revolution (1910–29) over more radical sectors emerging in the North (an alliance of radical, educated middle-class and urban and rural workers) and in the South (a popular revolutionary peasant movement) (Rueschmeyer et al. 1992:201).[5] Initially, victorious constitutionalist elites and sectors of the middle-classes formed an alliance with organized labor in 1917 to establish postrevolutionary control over the state apparatus and over the nation. Yet, they too were unable to consolidate a constitutionalist project in the face of regionally based armed challenges to the centralized government (1926–29). By 1929, the constitutionalist project had become transformed into an effort to centralize power, rather than to institutionalize contestation and widen political inclusion.

The centralized political structure that resulted solved the problem of stability in an anti-constitutionalist, corporatist direction. The founding of the PNR (National Party of the Revolution) (1928–38), the PRM (Party of the Mexican Revolution, 1938–46) under Lázaro Cardenas, and the PRI (Party of the Institutionalized Revolution) (since 1946) achieved stability by reducing the political power of local bosses, co-opting the military into participating in the political process and organizing peasants and organized workers hierarchically into the vertical sectors of a corporatist regime (Garrido 1982).

In structural terms, the twentieth-century Mexican regime, which began in 1917 as a constitutional settlement built upon the preeminence of the executive over the other branches of government, deteriorated into a unique Mexican-style authoritarianism (Garrido 1989:420). "Unwritten" laws, as opposed to the "written" laws contained in the Constitution, have endowed the executive with almost unlimited powers and functions including the ability to choose:

his successor, to act as a constituent power with the authority to make amendments to the Constitution, to act as chief legislator since historically senators and legislators have not legislated, to establishment himself as the ultimate authority in electoral matters since electoral material does not fall under the aegis of judicial review, to designate state governors, members of PRI majorities in Congress, and most state representatives and mayors, to remove governors, mayors and legislators at the federal and state levels, to impose his viewpoint on one or both houses of Congress, to assume jurisdiction in judicial matters, to impose his authority over state governors, and to hold sway over municipal governments. (Carpizo 1978; Garrido 1989:423–25)

The development of hypercentralism in the Mexican presidency and the use of meta-constitutional prerogatives has shaped the institutional expression of mass support and dissent in the twentieth-century Mexican presidential system (Cornelius et al. 1989:8). In comparative terms, Mexico's presidentialist system shares with modern authoritarian socialist regimes such as fascist Italy and the Soviet Union: (1) the vertical incorporation of sectors into corporations, (2) the selective use of repression and negotiation (Collier and Collier 1979), (3) an emphasis on the extension of social citizenship rights (basic wages, hours and working practices guaranteed by the state) over civil and political citizenship rights, (4) the domestication of the organized labor movement into controlled sectors, and (5) adherence to a revolutionary legitimating ideology (Gilly 1994). These attributes give the regime the label of "corporatist" and "authoritarian" but not Leninist.

On the other hand, the Mexican regime has never really historically delineated or persecuted "out-groups" such as property-owners. Indeed, members of the middle classes and capitalists who objected to the quasi-socialist corporatist structure of the regime during its consolidation phase have been tolerated as a formal right-wing opposition political party since 1939 (Partido Accion Nacional, or PAN). Over the course of the twentieth-century, the middle classes were incorporated into the regime structure (1950s) along with the earlier incorporation of peasants and workers (1930s). Also, the regime has had a mixed response to liberal legal rights. To be sure, the church's right to own real property was taken away in 1917 (constitutional article 27), some land reform occurred in the 1934–40 period, and foreign oil companies holdings were expropriated in 1938.[6] In later periods, the state came to control such basic industries as fertilizers, telephones, electricity, airlines, steel, and cooper (Camp 1993:41). Nevertheless, the regime has generally upheld individual liberal legal rights, including universal contract law and guarantees of property rights.[7] And, since the mid-1980s, the state has reversed its control over basic industries by selling them off to private hands at a rapid rate.[8]

Most importantly, the regime has not historically used violent repression to anywhere near the same degree as authoritarian socialist regimes, preferring to keep the party structure together by patronage, clientelism, corruption, and occasional violence.[9] Its ability to forge strong alliances with the military and capitalists and to pacifically co-opt potential opposition has lead to the pervasiveness of the PRI system at all levels of power (local, state, and federal). Indeed, its tenacious pervasiveness has led some to liken it to a complex "net-like organization" that defies traditional notions of government or state sovereignty (*Harvard Law Review* 1995). These attributes have led to the labeling of the regime until the late 1980s and early 1990s as a "mild," "civilian," "bureaucratic," and "inclusionary" authoritarianism (Cornelius et al. 1989:8; Cardoso 1979:46; Collier 1979:24).

SOCIOLOGICAL IMPLICATIONS: THE CORPORATE STRUCTURING OF INTERESTS

In the consolidation of Mexico's postrevolutionary state (1930–39), regime elites thought that the social conflicts of the transition to industrialization would be more effectively managed under a paternalist authoritarian regime than under a democratic regime. Both the "land-industry" and the "worker-capitalist" cleavages were organized by the Mexican state in a corporate manner. Under state tutelage (1934–40), the state created a corporate apparatus that would link the state and the party to both peasants and the working class in a way that sought to represent their interests and prevent either segment from mounting an independent challenge to the regime (Hamilton 1982). In the Mexican revolutionary nationalism that developed in the wake of the revolution, a sense of Mexican identity and a distrust of major powers, especially the United States, was tied to a strong, interventionist state with exceptional powers; this was an instance of the institutionalized revolution (Bartra 1989). It is particularly important for forms of political consciousness that Mexican corporatism sought to integrate all class interests with capitalist development (Monsivais 1978). In this way, nationalism was linked to an integrative strategy that sought to dampen class conflict.

The Mexican state's corporate shaping of social interests, cleavages, and forms of political consciousness has had important consequences for the social bases of democratization, causing them to differ from the modal patterns of the democratizing experience in Western Europe. In contrast to the West, for example, the Mexican working class did not develop as a social force, relatively independent of the state and thus a potentially strong democratizing social actor, as described by theorists of the Western democratizing experience (Rueschmeyer et al. 1992). Rather, organized labor in Mexico has continued to vote for the authoritarian party (the PRI) even in the face of high unemployment, inflation, and severe declines in real wages under government-imposed austerity measures in the 1980s and 1990s. Organized labor does not view an exit to the opposition left party as an option: Its leaders seek to maintain organizational control, and fear that if it does not support the PRI, it will lose labor legislation that guarantees its organizational authority through closed shops (Murrillo 1997:68). The leftist opposition party, the Party of the Democratic Revolution (PRD), supports independent unions and dissidents against the official union leaders; the rightist opposition party, the National Action Party (PAN), is unofficially linked to business. Until May 1999, when the Supreme Court overturned the labor unions' forced corporate affiliation to the PRI, the Mexican unionized working classes were even legally tied to the corporate structure of the state (*La Jornada* 1999).

Furthermore, the state's corporate organization led to a twentieth-century strategy of state-directed development, import-substituting industrialization, employed statism, and protectionism. These elements maintained this authoritarian political arrangement, led by a series of strong executives. Even Mexico's integration into a global market (1982 to the present) is under the leadership of an executive state elite committed to imposing a single, exclusive policy paradigm "based on the application of instrumentally rational techniques" (Centeno 1994:4). During the statist period, the Mexican rulers of the PRI relied on a series of implicit economic pacts with each of the major social groups in exchange for political support. Wilkie (1990:44) argues that 19 such implicit pacts existed. For example, farmers on small, communally owned farms obtained land redistribution, some credit, and stable agriculture prices for products; commercial cattle ranchers gained credit, exemption from land reform, and tacit government permission for growth; organized laborers obtained protection under labor laws and guarantees of minimum social rights; financial groups gained stable convertibility of pesos to dollars for investment abroad, protection against increasing the cost of the peso to amortize foreign debt, and protection against foreign investors' assuming more than 49 percent control of Mexican firms; and bureaucrats were assured a growing supply of jobs in the ever-expanding central and decentralized governments as well as benefits from social security, housing, and commissary and credit schemes. The "neoliberal" phase of Mexican economic development has included privatization of state-owned enterprises, has opened the economy to international competition, has overhauled the *ejido* (communally owned) land structure (Centeno 1994), and has begun dismantling these implicit pacts with society (Wilkie 1990:44, note 1).

One key consequence of authoritarian corporatism, especially the policy of employed statism, is that the economic fortunes of important sectors of the Mexican urban middle classes, such as civil servants, are linked inextricably to the well-being of the Mexican authoritarian state. Government employees (teachers, railroad workers, civil servants, and industrial workers in government-owned industries, such as miners, electricians, and petroleum workers) constitute fully one-third of organized labor in Mexico (Camp 1993:121). According to official government statistics, in Mexico City (the Federal District) approximately 22 percent of formally employed persons work for the state (INEGI 1990). In Mexico's 30 states, the proportion of this statist middle class varies from 10 percent in Chiapas to 22 percent in Baja California Sur (INEGI 1990). In addition, many intellectuals have histories of employment in public life: either in a federal bureaucracy, especially the secretariats of foreign affairs and education, or in various political posts as cabinet members, party leaders, and governors (Camp 1993:124).

This corporate social organization of important sectors of the urban middle classes also has brought consequences of democratization that differ from those of the Western experience. In the latter, the development of an anti-authoritarian urban middle class is hypothesized to be clearly related to higher levels of urbanization, education, and income (Lipset 1959:83). Mexico's urban middle classes, however, are politically divided three ways: pro-authoritarian, and favoring the right and the left democratic opposition. The ideological right includes an anti-authoritarian subgroup of the urban, educated, well-to-do middle class, which is antistatist and principally feels threatened by an inefficient and corrupt state (Alducin Abitia 1986; Loeza 1989:359–60, 1997:33). This subgroup differs from the faction on the democratizing left, which favors state intervention in the political and economic spheres, and generally supports egalitarian policies (Loeza 1989:359). Thus, one reason Mexico's transition to democracy is delayed relates to the complex, and politically divided role of the middle-classes which are simultaneously pro-authoritarian, and favoring the right and the left democratic opposition.

POLITICAL OPPOSITION PARTIES AND TUTELARY DEMOCRACY

Mexico's historical experience of a licensed or tolerated political opposition has also created institutional dynamics that have delayed the transition to democracy in comparison with the breakdown of military regimes in the third wave transitions.

Early on, in the wake of the Mexican Revolution, those on the ideological right who objected to the statist, populist economic policies of Lazaro Cardenas (1934–40) opted to peacefully challenge the corporate consolidation of the Mexican Revolution by the formation, in 1939, of the Party of National Action (PAN). The regime has tolerated this political opposition on the right, and the PAN has competed in every election since 1958. Initially and for most of its history until 1994, the PAN won only 10 to 20 percent, at most, of the national vote, in part because of its narrow regional, urban platform and in part because of election fraud (Loeza 1989; Mabry 1973; Mizrahi 1995). In the 1988 presidential election, the PAN garnered 17 percent of the votes cast (Nassif 1989:106); in the 1994 presidential election it won 26 percent (Klesner 1995:145).

The Mexican left initially was torn between those who advocated a revolutionary strategy of opposing one-party rule and those who opted to run in elections after the 1997 "political pact" expanded the regime's limited political pluralism by incorporating the nonrevolutionary left into the electoral arena (Middlebrook 1986).

In the period after 1977, the Mexican political left was fragmented into seven parties (Woldenburg 1997). This division delayed the formation of a single, coherent leftist party until the events of the late 1980s. In 1987, Carlos Salinas de Gortari, a clearly "technocratic" candidate, was nominated for the presidency by the PRI. Disgruntled PRI statist politicians claimed that the selection of de Gortari was "nothing but a disguised reelection which will perpetuate the rule by a counter-revolutionary clique . . . controlled by international financial interests" (Muñoz Ledo, quoted in Centeno 1994.2–13). They were expelled from the PRI and went on to challenge it by fielding a united leftist opposition front in the highly contested 1988 presidential election. The left claimed victory in an election that occurred in the face of widespread opposition claims of electoral fraud. From this front, a subsequent leftist political party, the Party of the Democratic Revolution (PRD), consolidated in 1989. The front won an official high of 31.06 percent of the national vote in the 1988 presidential elections; then the PRD's share declined to 16.60 percent in the 1994 presidential elections (Dresser 1998:57; Woldenburg 1997:44).

Mexico's transition to democracy in the 1990s is thus characterized by a dualistic opposition ideologically divided over differences in statist economic policies (Dominguez and McCann 1995). Historically the PAN has occupied a privileged position, at least as compared with the PRD, as the party more supportive of the government. After the 1988 presidential election, this situation led to a political "pact" in which the PAN leadership distanced itself from the PRD in 1989, and agreed to support President Salinas's economic privatization program in exchange for official recognition of its victories at the state and municipal levels (Crespo 1996; Pardinas and Amezcua 1997). The 1989 "pact" left the now-consolidated statist PRD outside the central circles of official power during the 1988–94 *sexenio*. In August 1994, upon the election of PRI President Zedillo, the PRI officially reconciled itself to the PRD in another "pact" aimed at reforming the state (Dresser 1998).

The 1994 presidential election also marks an important acceleration of democratization in Mexico because it has resulted in a comparatively rapid rise in the opposition parties' electoral fortunes. In the late 1980s and early 1990s, a few governorships were conceded to the right, but by 1996 only four of 30 governorships and the federal district were still in opposition (PAN) hands. By mid-1997, however, the PAN-PRD opposition controlled slightly over half of the nation's capital cities (*Reforma*, 7/13/98), 40 percent of all Senate seats (Amparo Cesar and de la Madrid 1998:42), and a majority of seats in the federal Chamber of Deputies (Lawson 1998:14). By mid-1998, the major opposition parties controlled about one-third of all state governorships and 44 percent of all municipalities (Amparo Cesar and de la Madrid 1998:43). By early 1999, the opposition vote represented 46 percent of the national vote share (28 percent PAN, 18 percent PRD) (Dresser 1999) and controlled ten of the 30 state legislatures (Amparo Cesar and de la Madrid 1998:43). In short, the electoral fortunes of the major political opposition parties increased significantly in the period from 1995 to 1999.

Nevertheless, the legacy of a divided political opposition party remains in the post-1994 period, as do the electoral laws facilitating continued divisions in the opposition. Under current law, enacted after the near triumph of the left in the 1988 presidential elections, a coalition can receive government campaign funding for only one party, even though any coalition is made up of more than one party, and even though both parties must follow only one party's ideological platform (Patterson 1999). Because parties receive most of their funding from the government, this law places any coalition at a severe disadvantage because two parties in a coalition receive funding for only one party. Opposition parties recently have made various unsuccessful efforts to change existing laws that discourage opposition coalition candidates (Peschard 1997; Schatz 1998). During the 1994–99 period, however, a joint PAN-PRD candidate has been fielded in relatively few elections (*Reforma* 1999).[10] Thus, the licensing of political opposition parties has delayed the transition to democracy by creating the uneven development of opposition parties; each gaining a stake in the electoral system at a different point in time by carving out its own ideological niche distinctive from the dominant single-party. Because opposition political parties are not strong enough alone to make a clean sweep of the institutions of the old regime, the transition to democracy is delayed.

THE DELAYED TRANSITIONS MODEL AND THE MEXICAN CASE VIEWED EMPIRICALLY

In this section, my aim is to demonstrate empirically, in a large scale empirical examination of over thirty-four thousand voters using logit regression analysis and in the examination of the attitudes among self-declared supporters of Mexico's three principal political parties, that one central consequence of state-led industrial development managed under a paternalist authoritarian regime is the development of voter alignments and democratizing forms of party organization and values reflective of authoritarian statism.

Toward this end, I make two predictions based on the delayed transitions model to explain the social patterns, structures, and process that make up the sociocultural bases of the transition. (1) I hypothesize that the Mexican case of democratization has revealed a dualistic anti-authoritarian voting coalition composed of an anti-authoritarian middle class and anti-authoritarian sectors of the nonprivileged classes who are not politically allied. This "dualistic, nonallied" democratizing mobilization has delayed the transition to democracy in Mexico because each democratizing class has pursued its own democratizing agenda through those political parties that represent it most successfully. (2) I also hypothesize that the one consequence of Mexico's policy of licensed opposition parties has included a distinctive nexus of cultural values for each of the three major political parties. I predict distinctive "pro-state" and "anti-statist" values, respectively, in the two major opposition parties, and the continued legitimacy of the regime in a large sector of the population. All of these factors have delayed the transition to democracy and inhibited clear democratizing alliances between opposition parties.

DATA, VARIABLES, MODELS, AND METHODS

I concentrate on the years 1991–97 because they frame the most important era of electoral democratization in Mexican history. Before the 1988 elections, the PRI claimed election victories virtually without fail (Gomez-Tagle 1994:240–42). The PRI has never accepted defeat in a presidential election. It had never accepted defeat for a Senate seat until 1988, or for a governorship until 1989. During the 1991–97 period, however, Mexico's electoral institutions began to ensure greater competitiveness. The political opposition slowly gained power such that the PAN-PRD opposition controlled slightly over half of all the capital cities of the nation by mid-1997 (*Reforma* 1998), 40 percent of all Senate seats (Amparo Cesar and de la Madrid 1998:42), and a majority of seats in the federal Chamber of Deputies (Lawson 1997:14).

The currency crisis of December 1994–January 1995, in which the peso lost over 50 percent of its value (Urzua 1997), is also a defining event of the 1991–97 period, which contributed to the acceleration of opposition voting. By examining voter alignments during this period, it is possible to explore the social bases of democratization under conditions of economic opening and political liberalization in Mexico's delayed transition to democracy.

Data. The study is based on a series of regional exit polls conducted in seven states and the Federal District throughout the 1990s (CIDE 1991; Giménez 1997). The polls, consisting of 34,121 personal interviews, were conducted in 1991–94 and 1997 on the following election days: July 7, 1991 (Nuevo Leon); July 10, 1992 (Michoacán); July 4, 1993 (México); September 26, 1993 (Coahuila); November 11, 1993 (Yucatán); March 20, 1994 (Morelos); November 20, 1994 (Tabasco); and July 6, 1997 (Federal District, Sonora, San Luis Potosí, Querétaro, Colima, Campeche, and Nuevo León). The polls were conducted by two independent polling agencies, Opinion Profesional, S.A. de C.V., a private company specializing in policy polling and focus groups (for the 1991–94 polls) and the investigative unit of *Reforma* (for the 1997 polls).

The interviews were distributed in proportion to each state's population. Cities, towns, and villages (with at least 1,000 residents) designated as polling locations were chosen randomly within each state, as follows: 98 locations in Michoacán; 51 locations in Nuevo León (in 1991); 85 locations in Mexico State; 57 locations in Coahuila; 110 locations in Yucatán; 69 locations in Morelos; 211 locations in Tabasco; 36 locations in Querétaro; 25 locations in San Luis Potosí; 18 locations in Colima; 21 locations in Sonora; and 20 locations in Campeche. In the Federal District, a random sample of one out of every 17 registered voters was constructed from the voters' registrer (*Reforma* 1998:7B). The margin of error is 3 percent to 5 percent over the thirteen elections. Exit poll interviews were conducted with persons over age 18, who were selected voluntarily as they left the polling place. Because it was expected that many respondents would be reluctant to express their voting intentions and political preferences, a simulated secret ballot procedure was employed for these questions. Respondents were asked to mark their preference on a sheet of paper, seal it, and place it in a box.

Variables. The measures of the first dependent variable used here are the votes for political parties in 1991–97. I regress these measures in separate equations, using logit regression analysis for each election on a series variables suggested by a review of the pertinent literature. The independent variables used to study the influence of economic development on voting patterns are standard demographic measures (age, sex, education), measures of economic development (rural-urban residence; *urban* is defined as cities with populations above 100,000), and measures of social class (defined by income and the occupational categories of government workers, private entrepreneurs, housewives, and agricultural workers).[11] I also included measures reflecting economic policy priorities: Respondents were asked whether they perceived that the current national economy had improved, stayed the same, or grown worse as compared with the previous year under PRI rule. Regional effects are controlled by using a representative sample of states covering northern, central, and southern regions. These states include Coahuila, Nuevo León, Sonora, and San Luis Potosí in the northern region; Morelos, México, Querétaro, Colima, Michoacán, and the Federal District in the central region; and Tabasco, Campeche, and Yucatán in the southern region.

The study also includes a second data panel of individual-level survey data on political culture gathered in 1991. I use this material to study the influence of sociopolitical values on support for the three political parties—PAN, PRD, and PRI—which again are the dependent variables. Here the independent variable used to study the influence of sociopolitical values on support for political parties include measures of values associated with democracy (democracy as associated with the concept of justice, liberty, order, and progress); measures of civic associationalism; measures of support for the rule of law; measures of individualism; and measures of collectivism.

Model and methods. I chose standard logistic regression with a bivariate dependent variable as the most effective method of analysis in this book. A bivariate dependent variable is used because I do not analyze each political party separately but rather I start from the assumption that Mexico's party system is a democratizing party system in this period with a single, dominant party and two principal, weaker opposition parties. A bivariate dependent variable has been employed in previous studies of the Mexican electorate (Centeno 1997:210; Dominguez and McCann 1995) because of the high rates of PRI voting in the early 1990s. It starts with the initial question of whether the individual would vote PRI or "other" party. The second assumption followed from the first: If the individual voted "other" party, or not PRI, which of the two opposition parties would he or she vote for—PAN or PRD?

RESULTS

Determinants of Party Choice and the Middle-Class Sectors

Table 2.1 presents multiple regression statistics of voting for democratic left (PRD), democratic right (PAN), and authoritarian (PRI) parties as a function of my 10 explanatory variables. I begin with an analysis of determinants of voters' choice for the PAN, the democratic political right party. My initial findings on voters' choice for the PAN appear to be consistent with previously established Western patterns of the social bases of democratization: anti-authoritarian opposition voting increases with the level of schooling, income, and urban status. Across all 13 elections throughout the 1990s where the PAN competed, I found a strong, positive, statistically significant relationship between for urban, educated, well-to-do status and a vote for the opposition PAN.

Thus the first conclusion is that the likelihood of rightist opposition voting is increased by higher levels of schooling, income, urban status, and (often) skepti-

Table 2.1
The Social Bases of Voter Alignments in Mexican Gubernatorial Elections, 1997

	Michoac. 1991			Nuevo Leon 1991		Mexico 1993			Coahuila 1993		Yucatan 1993		Morelos 1994			Tabasco 1994		Federal District 1997		
	PRI N=3288	PRD N=2018	PAN N=414	PRI N=4324	PAN N=2220	PRI N=3172	PRD N=308	PAN N=740	PRI N=1736	PAN N=716	PRI N=2293	PAN N=1147	PRI N=1840	PRD N=609	PAN N=244	PRI N=1194	PRD N=488	PRI N=546	PRD N=1438	PAN N=467
Urban	0.5708	-0.0000*	0.0000*	-0.0266*	0.0266*	0.7358	-0.5175	0.5175	-0.3223	0.8576	-0.0000*	0.0000*	-0.2366	-0.0000*	0.0000*	-0.0390*	0.0390*	N/A	N/A	N/A
Education	-0.0391*	-0.2179	0.0001*	-0.0000*	0.0000*	-0.0000*	0.3470	-0.3470	-0.0499*	0.0000*	-0.0007*	0.0007*	-0.0208*	-0.3337	0.2956	-0.9249	0.9249	-0.0004*	-0.0218*	0.0004*
Income	-0.4674	-0.0491*	-0.2101	-0.0000*	0.0000*	-0.0001*	-0.0000*	0.0008*	-0.0033*	0.1220	-0.0398*	0.0398*	0.2390	-0.0002*	0.0000*	0.0424*	-0.0422*	0.8578	-0.1593	0.0003*
Sex (M/F)	-0.0001*	0.0382*	-0.0000*	0.6230	-0.6230	-0.1496	0.4695	-0.4695	-0.5093	0.3742	-0.2913	0.2923	-0.1174	-0.3458	0.5139	-0.0037*	0.0037*	-0.2686	-0.0904	-0.9026
Age	-0.0001*	-0.0004*	0.7889	-0.0261*	0.0261*	-0.7307	-0.8174	0.4765	0.6949	-0.0293*	0.2405	-0.2405	-0.0724	-0.0654	0.6467	0.0064*	-0.0064*	0.0268*	0.7970	0.2137
Agricult.	0.0071*	0.0135*	-0.0333*	0.0000*	-0.0000*	...	...	...	—	—	—	—	—	—	—	—	—	—	—	—
Gov'L	0.0076*	0.0639*	-0.0000*	0.0000*	-0.0000*	0.3346	0.0228*	-0.0228*	0.0356*	-0.0115*	0.0011*	-0.0011*	0.3987	0.1436	-0.0276*	0.8851	-0.8851	0.0325*	0.0193*	-0.0151*
Business	0.0095*	-0.1986	0.0240*	-0.0277*	0.0277*	-0.7107	0.9024	-0.9024	0.5270	0.4772	-0.1693	0.1693	0.0573*	0.3427	0.4849	-0.9770	0.9770	0.3432	-0.0522*	0.0982+
H.Wives	0.0212*	0.3704	-0.5365	0.6510	-0.6510	0.4640	-0.4505	0.4505	0.0769	0.5103	0.2419	-0.2419	0.0654+	-0.8986	-0.8986	0.7948	-0.7948	0.0937+	-0.2838	0.0387*
EconEval	—	—	—	—	—	0.0000*	-0.0442*	-0.0442*	0.0000*	0.0000*	0.0000*	-0.0000*	0.0000*	-0.2388	0.9398	0.0000*	-0.0000*	0.0000*	-0.0000*	0.0001*

	Sonora 1997			Nuevo Leon 1997		Queretro 1997			Campche 1997		San Luis Potosi 1997		Colima 1997		
	PRI N=317	PRD N=173	PAN N=232	PRI N=268	PAN N=220	PRI N=279	PAN N=327	PT N=252	PRI N=497	PRD N=356	PRI N=299	PAN N=232	PRI N=275	PRD N=131	PAN N=205
Urban	0.0008*	0.8362	0.0326*	-0.0266*	0.0266*	0.7358	0.0028*	0.2409	-0.0000*	0.0566*	-0.6619	0.0002*	0.7304	0.6029	0.0305*
Education	0.0079*	-0.0839*	0.0552*	-0.0000*	0.0000*	0.0031*	0.0323*	-0.0648*	-0.0776*	0.0804*	0.7035	0.0593*	0.0243*	-0.3265	0.3023
Sex (M/F)	0.5726	-0.4567	0.5791	-0.0000*	0.0000*	0.2604	-0.0138*	0.2250	0.5861	0.8587	-0.0398*	-0.0434*	0.0744	-0.0860*	0.1348
Age	0.1547	-0.5609	0.8262	0.6230	-0.6230	-0.9274	-0.7528	0.4035	0.7161	-0.3136	0.0193*	-0.0534*	0.0008*	-0.0470*	-0.0074*
EconEval	0.0008*	0.4508	0.6626	-0.0261*	0.0261*	0.0000*	-0.0017*	0.4229	0.0000*	-0.0000*	0.0000*	-0.0508*	0.0005*	0.3032	-0.0424*

N = 34,121 (CIDE 1994, 1997; Giménez 1997): *0.05; +0.1.

cism toward the national economic consequences of the authoritarian regime's economic policies. Economic development is related positively to anti-authoritarian voting on the ideological right. These initial results appear to conform to macrosociological predictions on the role of the urban, educated, middle classes in the Western social bases of democratization (Przeworski and Limongi 1997). They also support previous ecological research which has found strong positive correlations between urban, industrialized districts with concentrations of literate voters and PAN electoral support (Klesner 1995).

Nevertheless, because the Mexican regime has brought significant numbers of people into these classes through state-sector employment, one sees that the urban, educated Mexican middle classes are split politically. An examination of government workers' voting alignments shows state-dependent civil servants voting for both the incumbent authoritarian regime and the democratizing statist left party in Michoacán (1991), México State (1993), and the Federal District (1997).

The findings suggest that support for statism and statist policies governs middle-class government workers' voting choices in two ways. First, in each of the elections, government workers' support for the democratic left statist PRD is high and stable. This support for the PRD by civil servants is correlated positively with the view that the regime's neoliberal economic policies have exerted a negative effect on the nation's current economy.

This finding dovetails with Kaufman and Zuckerman's (1998:366–67) results of the positive relationship between public sector employment and support for the regime's neo-liberal policies (measured by their "policy" and "general support indexes") in the 1992 and 1994 but not 1995 elections. Kaufman and Zuckerman (1998:366–67) also find the same relationship among high income and high levels of education, that is, that in the 1992 and 1994 elections, highly educated, well-to-do social status was a positive predictor of policy support for neoliberal economic reforms but not in 1995 after the peso crises.[12] In other words, government workers, as well as the educated, well-to-do voters' support for the PRI, was closely related to their perception of the effects of neoliberal economic policies.

Second, I find a highly statistically significant negative relationship between the civil servant occupation and a vote for the democratic right opposition party (PAN); this relationship also reveals a clear rejection of political parties ideologically sympathetic to reductions in statist policies. That is to say, members of the statist middle classes reject parties such as the PAN, which advocated cutting the number of state employees, reducing government spending and price controls, and curtailing the existence of public enterprises and state interventionism in the market (Loeza 1997:33).

This general relationship of the split, urban, educated middle classes and Mexican political parties is demonstrated clearly in Table 2.2. The data reveal that between 57 and 75 percent of the middle class supported the incumbent authoritarian regime in 1991–94; the opposition split the rest. In the states of Mexico (1993) and Morelos (1994), as a pertinent example, over 70 percent of the middle-class citizens supported the PRI in elections.[13]

Table 2.2
Split Middle-Class Vote by Mexican States, 1991-97

	Michoacan 1991 (N=2542)	Nuevo Leon 1991 (N=3055)	Yucatan 1993 (N=1847)	Mexico 1993 (N=4220)	Morelos 1994 (N=1494)	DF 1997 (N=1343)
PRI	57.1%	67.7%	63.0%	75.0%	70.48%	25.5%
PRD	34.3%	2.2%	0.7%	7.6%	21.8%	58.8%
PAN	8.6%	30.1%	36.6%	16.0%	7.6%	15.5%

Includes income categories of 1-3 and 3-5 times monthly minimum wage.

Table 2.3
Split Middle-Class Vote by Mexican States, 1997

	Sonora 1997 (N=511)	Nuevo Leon 1997 (N=418)	S.L. Potosi 1997 (N=314)	Queretaro 1997 (N=529)	Colima 1997 (N=448)	Campeche 1997 (N=579)
PRI	35.4%	35.9%	28.3%	24.8%	27.1%	44.6%
PRD	16.8%	—	6.7%	7.0%	12.9%	35.2%
PAN	23.7%	64.1%	29.8%	24.6%%	24.6%	8.3%

Includes education categories of secondary, university and above.
Where percentages do not sum to 100%,
the remaining vote share was won by the
semi-opposition parties.

These results lead to my first conclusion about the social bases of the breakdown and democratization in Mexico. Certainly my findings support the positive relationship between democracy and economic development, as carried by some sectors of the urban middle class. Nevertheless, civil servants' dependence on the authoritarian state diminishes the overall importance of the urban, educated middle class as the key democratizing social actors in Mexico; the importance of this class was predicted both by the modernization theory of Lipset et al. (1993) and by the class-analytic model of Rueschmeyer et al. (1992) as applied to the Mexican case.

Theoretically this finding of a divided middle class is significant because it shows how the transition to democracy is delayed by countervailing sources of middle-class support for the authoritarian regime. In states where a high percentage of the urban middle class is employed in the state sector, the strength of the educated, urban, statist middle class in favor of authoritarianism can be a significant cause of delay. The Mexican middle classes cannot be theorized as the leading carriers of the democratizing struggle, as suggested by structural theorists. Instead these middle sectors must be theorized as an internally complex social force whose preferences can not easily be theorized as predominantly anti-authoritarian.

Determinants of Party Choice and Competitive Elections

Table 2.3 reveals the old single party's capacity to continue winning elections even in an increasingly competitive electoral environment. The data show that in the July 1997 election, the single party survived electorally despite a decline in support from the middle classes. The PRI won four of the six contested governorships (66 percent) in the July 1997 elections (Sonora, Querétaro, Colima, Campeche), even in the most highly contested elections in the nation's history.

This durability on the part of the old single party is largely a product of the continued political division between the major opposition parties. In the 1997 Sonora election, for example, the PRI won the governorship with support from only 35 percent of the middle class because the political opposition remained divided politically. Taken together, the opposition parties (PRD, PAN) could have won 40.5 percent of the combined middle-class vote in Sonora. Similarly, in the 1997 Colima election, the PRI won the governorship with support from only 27 percent of the middle class because the major political opposition was politically divided: In combination, PAN and PRD accounted for 37.5 percent of the middle-class vote.

These findings on the voting patters of the urban, educated middle class also support the theoretical assertion that the electoral survival of a single party in an increasingly competitive electoral climate is a feature of delayed transition to democracy. Political divisions within the opposition parties not only divide the opposition vote of the urban, educated, well-to-do, but also reflect a pattern of social cleavages: party alignments in which this class is not the major anti-authoritarian social force.

Determinants of Party Choice and the Nonprivileged Sectors

In fact, Mexico's delayed transition to democracy has also involved a sustained effort to mobilize the nonprivileged classes on the political left. The data in Table 2.1 also reveal the slow emergence of an alternative rural-urban poor social coalition, as evidenced in the PRD's ability to capture the votes of the rural poor (Michoacán 1991), the poor (Mexico 1993), the urban poor (Tabasco 1994), and the less highly educated (Mexico City 1997) (Lawson 1998:16),[14] as against the traditional populist social coalition of the PRI. Although the PRI maintains sectors of its traditional coalition (Klesner 1995; Gibson 1997:351)—the less highly educated (Michoacán 1991, Mexico City 1997) (Magaloni 1998:228),[15] the less highly educated poor (Mexico 1993) (Poiré 1998:38),[16] and rural voters (Tabasco 1994)—its electoral hegemony has been challenged by the democratic left throughout the 1990s.

More important, the data reveal that a major difference between the nonprivileged PRI and PRD voters is their perception of the effects of neoliberalism on the Mexican economy. Wherever the nonprivileged classes are divided, the PRI vote is explained by a positive perception of these effects (Mexico 1993, Tabasco 1994, Federal District 1997, Campeche 1997), whereas the PRD vote is explained by a negative assessment (Mexico 1993, Tabasco 1994, Federal District 1997, Campeche 1997). Poor voters' assessment of the national economic consequences of neoliberalism was translated into party support in opposite ways. In a parallel view, Buendía (1996:567, 578–79) has found that social class played a mediating role between economic conditions and PRI presidential approval in the 1989-1993 period. He found that Salinas' ratings were highest among high-income people and lowest among low-income people. I would qualify Buendía's finding from 1989–1993 to add that low-income people are split politically; those voting PRD rate the economic consequences of Salinas's neoliberal economic policies negatively; those voting PRI, even if poor, rated the economic consequences of Salinas's neoliberal policies positively.

My findings lead to a second conclusion about the social bases of the breakdown of Mexico: It strongly suggests that the mobilization of the popular class requires a concomitant strong rejection of the incumbent regime's neoliberal position because the original populist base of the authoritarian regime fragments and delays the popular mobilization of the rural-urban poor who oppose it.[17]

Overall these empirical results on the social bases of voters' alignments support my initial hypothesis that the Mexican case of democratization involves both the anti-authoritarian middle class and sectors of the nonprivileged classes who perceive themselves as excluded from the benefits of Mexico's economic development strategies. This "dualistic, non-allied" democratizing mobilization is delaying the transition to democracy in Mexico because actors in each of these classes pursue distinct democratizing agendas through the political parties that they believe represent their interests most effectively.

So far I have examined empirically the material interests that cause and delay the transition to democracy in Mexico. Theoretically, to avoid reductionism to material interests alone, it is necessary to illustrate how such interests are intertwined with culturally derived notions of democracy and relations between the state and civil society. Thus, to show the legacy of "tutelary" democracy on mass beliefs and the organization of political parties, I now discuss the findings on the second distinguishing feature of Mexico's delayed transition to democracy: legitimation and the nature of the links between state and civil society.

Political Attitudes and Mexico's Delayed Transition to Democracy

The findings from Table 2.4 reveal several interesting political attitudes reflective of the Mexican regime's policy of limited political pluralism and semicompetitive elections at the mass level of political participation. A very high proportion of survey respondents (78 percent) have voted in Mexico, while a large majority of the population contains those who are not members of civic associations: 83 percent of the survey respondents did not belong to any social organization or group in 1991. Furthermore, a majority of the population did not have a clear sense of collective action when asked about the ways in which they would stand up for their political ideas. These results suggest that historically, voting has been the major form of political participation, and that before the late 1980s and early 1990s, membership in civic organizations was not widespread.

The public opinion findings also reveal several interesting aspects of the past and present legitimacy of the authoritarian populist single party. On one hand, survey respondents perceived that it was difficult to participate in politics (67 percent). On the other hand, however, a very large majority perceived the government as legitimate in regard to upholding basic constitutional rights of association: 75 percent thought the Salinas government guaranteed basic rights of association, and 68 percent thought it guaranteed basic freedoms of speech. The findings also reveal the historical legacy of the regime, namely a lack of focus on class in the majority of the population. Sixty-three percent of those surveyed thought the government serves the interests of the people; only 8 percent believed that the government serves the interests of the "rich" or the "bourgeoisie."

In other words, respondents did not judge the government as illegitimate or as tied to the interests of an elite majority. Instead the 1991 results reveal that the government is legitimate on the basic dimensions of civil rights; they also suggest a relatively demobilized populace habituated to voting but feeling distant from its leaders.

Citizens' mobilization in Mexico City has increased dramatically since 1994 as the electoral success of opposition political parties and democratization has accelerated (GEA Político 1996; Latin American Data Base 1997:4–5). Indeed, this wave of increased social mobilization, in combination with more freedom in the news media, helps to explain the surge of support for the PRD in the Mexico City election of July 1997 (Lawson 1998).

Yet the 1991 findings regarding political attitudes also confirm another legacy of the relations between the state and civil society in Mexico's delayed transition to democracy: They show the success of the "tutelary democracy" legitimation

Table 2.4
State-Civil Society Linkages in Mexico (N = 6,990)

Since the age of 18, have you voted?	**Yes 78.5%** No 16.5%
Do you belong to any type of social organization or groups?	**No 83.2%** Yes 15.4%
Type of organization?	Union 3.3% Political Party 3.4% Religious 3.3% Neighborhood 1.7% Professional 0.9% Other 2.8%
Is it hard or easy to participate in politics?	**Hard 67%** Easy 16% D/K 16%
Does the current government guarantee basic freedom of association? Basic freedom of speech?	**Yes 75.1%** No 5.4% D/K 17.1% **Yes 67.9%** No 12.9% D/K 17.2%
Do opposition parties compete with the same opportunities to gain power?	**Yes 50.9%** No 28.0% D/K 18.4%
Do you think that the current government serves the interests of all the people or only those of a single group?	The people 63.3% Single group 20.9% D/K 14.4% No Answer 1.4%
If a single group, which one?	**The rich/bourgeoisie/ 7.8%** **businessmen** Those with political 5.5% power Other 4.1% D/K 3.5%
In what way(s) would you stand up for your political ideas?	**D/K 50.1%** No Answer 13.8% Collective Action 8.1% Voting/Parties 8.1% Dialogue 7.7% Other 12.2%

	USA	UK	China	Mexico
Which of the following countries has a democratic government? Yes	44%	22%	14.5%	**54%**
No	13%	19%	23%	15%
D/K	44%	60%	62%	31%

Note: D/K means "do not know."
Source: CIDE 1991.

strategy in shaping mass beliefs in the democratic intentions of Mexico's rulers. Despite a legacy of institutionalized election fraud in the 1970s, 1980s (Camp 1993:62, 152; Loeza 1985), and early 1990s (Centeno 1994:225–27), more than half of the population surveyed already believed in 1991 that the opposition parties compete with the same opportunities to gain power as does the incumbent authoritarian regime (28 percent replied "do not know"). A majority of the population also classified Mexico as possessing a democratic form of government. These 1991 findings are further confirmed by studies of cultural attitudes in 1997, which showed that a majority of middle-class Mexican citizens in major cities also believed that the Mexican political system was already democratic (Aguayo 1999; Meyer 1998; Rivapalacio 1998).

These findings lead to the following paradox: Although opposition political elites historically have struggled to reduce inequalities in campaign resources, to increase access to the media, and to reduce vote buying by the party-state, many in the population think the nation is already democratic, as defined in terms of fair and equitable conditions of competition for political office. This point suggests a conflict between democratizing elites and mass social actors in interpreting basic defining properties of democracy and democratization. It speaks to the rulers' continuing ability to convince the majority of its citizens of its concern for their social welfare and its commitment to furthering "democracy." As a result, most Mexicans perceived in the early 1990s that democracy already existed in Mexico. In 1991, however, a majority of academics classified the Mexican political system as "authoritarian" (Cornelius et al. 1989:8).

The following comparative argument can be made from these data on the nature of the links between the state and civil society. In the breakdown of military regimes, civil society groups such as human rights organizations and democratizing actors resurrect themselves into an "us versus them" dichotomy during the popular upsurge that occurs in the transition to democracy (O'Donnell and Schmitter 1986:54–55). Unlike the breakdown of military rule, Mexico's delayed transition to democracy is not marked by "us versus them," but by two distinct political opposition parties, a variety of social movements, and a quasi-populist regime with historical legitimacy in which a majority of the population believes that a democratic system is already in place.

Hence the sociological question of Mexico's transition to democracy is twofold: What attitudes lead mass actors to decide to vote in large numbers for the opposition? What attitudes cause mass actors to continue to support the old regime?

The Distribution of Political Attitudes among Self-Declared Supporters of the Three Principal Parties

The distribution of political attitudes among self-declared supporters of the three principal parties suggest that mass opposition voting in Mexico coincides with the dual mobilization of individuals on the right, organized into neighborhood associations, and the mobilization of an anti-neoliberal, statist center-left. Such mobilization occurs because of individuals' continued tendency to support the incumbent authoritarian regime and because of the single party's capacity to survive into the competitive phase of elections. To elaborate on this argument, I refer to Table 2.5, in which I regress a series of values on the dependent variable of support for different political parties.

The data in Table 2.5 reveal the values that explain opposition status. On the ideological right, the results show that PAN party supporters favor individual effort over collective effort as the preferred way of advancing oneself economically. PAN supporters also are highly involved in neighborhood associations. On the left, the results suggest that support for the opposition PRD is explained by mobilization into an opposition political party and by rejection of the incumbent authoritarian government's turn to neoliberal economic policy.

One conclusion that emerges from the data is that forms of civic associationalism (neighborhood-based organizations and political party mobilization) are central in explaining the rise of opposition support in Mexico's delayed transition to democracy. This finding supports a large body of previous work on the importance of civic associationalism for democratic forms of participation (Diamond 1994:4; Huntington 1994:202–3; Lipset [1960] 1981:52–53; Lipset et al. 1956; Merkl 1993; Rueschmeyer et al. 1992; Stephens 1993:414; Tocqueville 1976: vol. 2:116).

A second conclusion relates to the role of law as a source of regime legitimation. Belief in the legality of the regime is a central cultural source of legitimation. According to the data, PRI or government party supporters believed that the law was useful in Mexico. This finding regarding the centrality of law is consistent with the argument that belief in the legality, customs, and conventions associated with rulers is a central subjective determinant for the bases of the legitimacy of a given political order (Weber 1978:38). Belief in the importance of law is a "state-reinforcing" idea (Mann 1993:235) because the state is primarily responsible for upholding the rule of law.

Finally, economic factors again explain support for the single party: Voters supported the government's neoliberal economic reforms as a successful policy measure to improve the nation's economy. These positive perceptions of effects on the national economy, however, were not associated with the perception that the voters' own economic situation improved during that period. This finding supports previous research showing that views of general economic conditions are consistently stronger predictors of support for reform than are perceptions of personal well-being (Kaufman and Zuckermann 1998:365; Kiewiet and Kinder 1981). Definitions of democracy (as associated with the values of justice, liberty, order, or progress) were not statistically significant as determinants of support either for the opposition or for the regime.[18]

THE MEXICAN CASE IN THEORETICAL PERSPECTIVE

The Mexican findings suggest that theoretical emphasis, in political modernization accounts, on transformative industrialism and on its linkage to a linear

Table 2.5
The Ideological Structure of Mexican Party Support

	PRI (N=1161)	PAN (N=286)	PRD (N=903)
CIVIC ASSOCIATIONALISM			
Member Neighbor Assoc.	0.6936	0.0372*	0.9953
Member Political Party	0.7196	-0.3727	0.0699*
POPULISM vs. RULE OF LAW			
Law is Useful in Mexico	0.0019*	0.4404	-0.4917
Education	-0.1009	-0.3530	-0.7692
COLLECTIVISM vs. INDIVIDUALISM			
Gov't vs. Individual Effort	0.0004*	0.0510*	-0.4814
CONCEPT OF DEMOCRACY			
Democracy: Justice	0.7414	0.5792	0.9655
Democracy: Liberty	0.8550	-0.9211	0.8783
Democracy: Order	0.3903	-0.8902	0.2772
Democracy: Progress	0.6043	-0.9458	-0.9630
STATISM vs. NEOLIBERALISM			
Agree with Gov't Neoliberal Reforms	0.0000*	0.8750	-0.0009*
Economic Situation Improved in Last Year	0.2302	0.2119	0.4138

Source: CIDE 1991 (*N* = 2,350).

pattern of political cleavages (center-periphery, church-state, land-industry, capitalist-worker) is modeled too closely on the Western European democratizing experience to adequately explain Mexico's delayed transition to democracy. Similarly, the theoretical emphasis on the necessary democratizing capacities of the formal working class is linked too closely to the second wave of democratization in Western Europe to adequately explain the Mexican case. In Mexico, sectors of the formal working class and the lower middle classes have not united in a democratizing social coalition; such unification would be expected according to the logic of class-analytic theory, given relatively high rates of industrialization and the most severe global decline of wages under structural adjustment policies (Geddes 1994:65).[19] Despite the perception, among the majority of PAN and PRD voters, that the regime's neoliberal economic policies have failed, a democratizing opposition social coalition of the urban and rural poor, disgruntled government workers, and members of the urban sector hit hard by structural adjustment policies has yet to definitively emerge (Murillo 1997:68). That is, a united middle-class/working class democratizing coalition has not emerged in Mexico by 1997 although the prevailing economic conditions have been conducive to the formation of such a coalition.

Mexican society is characterized by uneven economic development: It possesses a growing tertiary sector in the metropolitan areas and in the north, which may explain the anti-regime vote among the educated, urban, well-to-do citizens.[20] Tertiary-sector growth, however, also causes civil service expansion and partially explains the opposite phenomenon: pro-regime voting. Industrialization and urbanization processes have created a large segment of urban poor persons willing to vote both for and against the regime, whereas the formal working class makes up less than approximately 10 percent of the formal working population (INEGI 1995). Finally, the continued importance of agrarianism in certain states has not necessarily been antithetical to democratization (Crenshaw 1995), as macrosociological theorists have argued (Moore 1966:420; Rueschmeyer, et al. 1992:2). Organizational factors matter, as Rueschmeyer et al. (1992:217–18) observe: The results from the state of Michoacán (1991) show that when a democratic left alternative exists, peasants split their vote between the authoritarian left PRI and the democratic left PRD.

The Mexican findings of voters' alignments strongly suggest that the social organization of both structural interest cleavages and collective political values in Mexico are shaped by a corporate historical and institutional pattern different from the Western democratizing experience and not consistent with the various theories on the Western European experience. As discussed more fully in chapter 1, in Mexico (Yates 1981) as in other societies in which the "land-industry/rural-urban" social cleavage historically did not translate into a political conflict between conservatives (landed interests) and liberals (the rising class of urban industrial entrepreneurs) (Lipset and Rokkan [1967]1985:134; Luebbert 1991), the interest situations of either workers or the middle classes differ from those of the Western European democratizing experience. The development of a "catch-all" party during the industrial phase of development in Mexico and Latin America (Dix 1989:27), rather than the "class/mass" parties of Western Europe (Lipset and Rokkan [1967] 1985:134; Luebbert 1991) meant that electoral support was achieved from a broad spectrum of voters that extended the party's reach well beyond that one of social class or religious denomination. The catch-all party developed ties to a variety of interest groups instead of exclusively relying on the organization and mobilizational assets of one (such as labor unions) (Dix 1989:26–27). As aforenoted, specifically, Mexico's "catch-all" PRI party-state reflects a particular quasi-leftist, historical legacy in which the social conflicts of the transition to industrialization were believed to be managed most effectively under a paternalist, authoritarian, corporate regime.

The social alignments of interests in the breakdown of corporatism in Mexico of the 1990s have revealed a pattern of simultaneous, but non-allied, mobilization in which the anti-authoritarian middle classes and sectors of the nonprivileged classes do not unite into a single democratizing front. The Mexican findings show that economic development and democracy are related positively and that this relationship is carried by the anti-authoritarian middle classes, as suggested by theories of the Western European democratizing experience. Nevertheless, significant sectors of the middle classes still firmly support the authoritarian regime; thus the middle classes are deeply divided politically. This point strongly suggests that the middle classes are not the leading carriers of democratization in Mexico.

Rather, the Mexican case of democratization reveals that the central democratizing actors are both the anti-authoritarian middle class and sectors of the nonprivileged classes who disagree with Mexico's neoliberal economic development strategy. As the result of the legacy of the corporate structuring of interests and forms of political consciousness, each democratizing social sector pursues its own distinctive democratizing agenda through those political parties that represent them most effectively. This "dualistic, non-allied" democratizing mobilization delays the transition to democracy in Mexico by constraining the development of a united middle-class/working-class democratizing coalition. Mexico's delayed transition to democracy can be explained not by the failure of anti-authoritarian middle classes or nonprivileged classes to mobilize but by their inability or unwillingness to ally politically.

Certain forms of political consciousness, shaped by the successful legitimation strategy of "tutelary democracy," also delay the transition to democracy. The "pro-statist" and "anti-statist" values that explain support for opposition parties reflect distinctive mass beliefs that are the legacy of the institutionalization of a party system with licensed opposition parties. The opposition parties' willingness to participate electorally with the regime has led to the slow development of opposition leadership organization and to an increasingly competitive electoral environment. Yet the dominant party's capacity to continue winning elections even in the newly competitive electoral environment suggests that it possesses a social base of support and retains elements of control over the electoral system.

At the level of mass beliefs, more than half of all respondents apparently believe that voting and the existing system of party competition in Mexico are evidence that Mexico is already a democratic system. A majority of respondents also appeared to believe that the government was legitimate in its upholding of constitutional liberties of speech and association. Given that the dominant party continues to be the most important single political force in the nation, these mass beliefs support the idea that a strategy of "tutelary democracy" has been successful as a form of regime legitimation. A long-term strategy of limited political pluralism and semicompetitive elections apparently has created, in many citizens, the belief that continued political participation through voting will lead one day to the creation of a democratic regime (Loeza 1985:80; Scott 1965:330–95, 371). One voter seemed to suggest this when summarizing the state of democratization in Mexico in 1998 stated, "Before it didn't matter much whether we voted or not, but now the people themselves are reforming Mexico, and that has made it matter" (Dillon 1998:2).

The strategy of slow, gradual democratization supervised and guided by the dominant party reflects a pattern unlike that found in the breakdown of military regimes. In most transitions from military rule, the relatively heterogeneous political opposition managed to unite, if only temporarily, into a broad social coalition demanding political rights. In Spain, for example, the democratizing opposition of Christian Democrats, regional parties, liberals, Social Democrats, Socialists, Communists, illegal unions, and members of Catalan, Basque, and Galician oppositions fused into a single coalition and converged on a joint program of formal political rights as a condition for consenting to negotiate with the regime ("A un Paso" 1976; Carr and Fusi 1981).[21] Another such example of unification occurred in Chile, in the joint constitutional proposals, made in 1980, by a heterogeneous social coalition of Christian Democrats, Communists, and Socialists and in the 1983 "national protests" by heterogeneous organizations such as the urban poor and other politically organized groups (Garreton 1992:113–17). After the transition to democracy, virtually none of the organizations of the military have continued to play a central political role (Cruz and Diamint 1998:116).

In contrast, the widespread belief that democracy already exists in Mexico demonstrates the continued legitimacy of the dominant party as the "midwife" of democracy. The transition to democracy is delayed by the capacity of the PRI to continue winning elections when more than 50 percent of the educated, well-to-do electorate vote for the opposition, and by the legal-economic barriers that inhibit coalition candidates in non-Leninist single-party regimes.

CONCLUSION

The social alignments analyzed in this chapter reflect the particular pattern of the breakdown of Mexico's non-Leninist authoritarian single-party system. This chapter has identified political divisions within the social base of the opposition parties as a singularly important dimension causing delay in the Mexican transition to democracy. This analysis strongly suggests that the successful unification of opposition parties can be predicted to significantly and rapidly accelerate the Mexican transition to democracy. By August 1999, the Mexican rightist and leftist opposition parties signed a pathbreaking formal agreement to potentially field a joint candidate for the 2000 presidential race in light of continued public opinion polls suggesting the PRI would likely win the presidency if the political opposition remained divided politically (El Mundo 1999).[22] The success of this political unification will depend importantly on the general desire of Mexican citizens for accelerated democratic change. With 81% of the population surveyed in 1991 wanting social change to occur slowly, "little by little" (Giménez 1997), a rapid, clean sweep of the old party from most of the posts of power remains unlikely.

Democracy is a multidimensional set of institutional structures whose central dimensions include the separation of powers and the extension of the franchise that make up the structural configuration of the state (Dahl 1989:221; Collins 1998).[23] Because each of these institutional dimensions is a continuum, not an-all-or-nothing condition (Collins 1998:15), it is not surprising that in the post–1994 period, several other interrelated democratizing transformations of Mexican society, and its political and legal institutions were taking place along this continuum. Democratizing social actors in the 1990s were attempting to: (1) expand the Mexican Supreme Court's powers of judicial review and to increase the autonomy of Mexico's electoral institutions from centralized control (1994–96), and (2) to transformation of the Chamber of Deputies from a party-state controlled body into an opposition controlled one after the historical 1997 elections.

The delayed transitions model predicts that democratization involves the continual, ongoing, social struggle over the incremental extension of political rights; and the effort to disperse decision-making power to a wider number of actors not affiliated with the party-state in collective decision-making bodies (electoral bodies, legislatures, independent judiciaries, federalism). Chapter 3 begins the analysis of these social struggles with a discussion of the historical, centralized executive control over elections and the checking of the legitimacy of electoral outcomes before turning to an empirical analysis of the slow expansion of judicial review and of legislative autonomy.

NOTES

1. At the same time, democratization brought a series of less rosy changes including a rise in crime, an increase in the number of reported shipments of drugs across Mexican territory, and the continuation of human rights violations (Hellman 1997:92).

2. The full historical explanation involves such variables as the intensity and length of the war of independence that left the military and the church as the only two institutionalized bases of power, repeated local rebellions, the war with the United States, and the French invasion, all of which strengthened the use of military forces as the major means to exercise and to resist political power (Meyer and Sherman, 1983). It was not until Diaz seized power that a monopoly of organized force could be established and state power could be centralized.

3. By 1996, the Mexican Supreme Court continued to uphold a definition of political rights that originated in 1882. In this definition, the Court removed political rights from constitutional review despite their protection under habeas corpus provisions granted in the 1857 constitution. The specific historical background of the legal developments of the rule of law and political rights are treated in greater detail later.

4. The Porfirio Diaz dictatorship ruled in Mexico from 1877 to 1880, and 1884 to 1911. Diaz used state power to maintain political order and to allow free reign to foreign investments (Coatsworth 1983:208–9; Meyer et al. 1994). Coatsworth examines the Moore thesis for the Porfiriato, and analyzes the central role of the state, arguing that this and the revolution created the conditions for the establishment of the modern corporatist authoritarian regime (1983:216).

5. Instead, the dominant classes helped to bring about the revolution, alienated by the increasing rigidity and corruption, equivocal support by the U.S. government, and the refusal of Diaz to allow for succession (Rueschmeyer et al. 1992:201–2).

6. This involved President Lazaro Cardenas's expropriation of the largely U.S.-owned oil industry in 1938. For detailed accounts of this historical event and of the reaction of the oil companies, see Townsend 1952. The maximum total land redistribution as ejido grant in Mexico was 11.2 percent before the revolution (1900–34) and 17.9 percent after the revolution (1934–40) (Roett 1995:42).

7. A caveat to this is the procedure of the PRI to involuntarily force the party membership of certain economic groups (taxi drivers, construction workers, etc.) in order for them to receive state regulatory licenses for their economic activities. This forced corporate membership does formally violate the liberal conception of the freedom of labor. The overturning of this practice is one of the changes brought about by the 1996 reforms (*La Jornada*, August 21, 1996:1).

8. Privatization of state-owned industries increased by 80 percent between 1987 and 1992. The state owned 1,155 firms but retained control of only 286 in 1992 (Mexico Report, 2/10/92:6).

9. The massacres of students in 1968 are the great exception to this rule. And, not surprisingly, this act of repression generated a entire generation of dissident youth, intellectuals, and not a few violent guerrilla movements (Meyer 1994:169–71).

10. The recent gubernatorial election in the state of Nayarit (1999) represents a departure from this pattern. In August 1999, the Mexican rightist and leftist opposition parties signed a formal agreement to potentially field a joint candidate for the 2000 presidential race in light of continued public opinion polls suggesting the PRI would likely win the presidency if the political opposition remained divided politically (El Mundo 1999). Yet, the success of this political unification will depend importantly on the general desire of Mexican citizens for accelerated democratic change. With 81 percent of the population surveyed in 1991 wanting social change to occur slowly, "little by little" (Giménez 1997), a rapid, clean sweep of the old party from most of the posts of power remains unlikely.

Furthermore, it should be noted that this potential unification does not imply the attainment of a "working-class-middle-class" democratizing social coalition (Rueschmeyer et al. 1992) because PRD supporters do not constitute the formal working class as defined by theories of transformative industrialization; and many PAN supporters are members of the "upper classes" or those individuals with the highest levels of education and wealth, as I argue in detail below for the 1991–94 data and with the highest levels of education for the 1997 data.

11. The *Reforma* 1997 surveys for the states of Colima, Nuevo Leon, Campeche, Sonora, Queretaro, and San Luis Potosi omit occupational and income variables (CIDE 1997).

12. In their OLS models, they find also income and Mexico City residence are statistically significant sociodemographic variables for predicting policy preferences about economic reform in the 1994 election but not in 1992 and 1995 elections (Kaufman and Zuckerman 1998:366-67).

13. Support for authoritarianism from the well-to-do (the upper bourgeoisie) was also hypothesized in the Southern Cone Latin American "bureaucratic-authoritarian states" of the 1970s (O'Donnell 1979:292–303).

14. Lawson (1998: 166) found that lower social class status (and male gender) were statistically significant positive predictors of PRD opinion and high education levels were a statistically significant positive predictor of PAN opinion in his analysis of the principal determinants of support for major Mexican Parties in the 1997 election in the Federal District.

15. Magaloni (1998:228) found low education and peasant status were clear positive predictors of PRI voter choice in the 1994 Presidential election in both her statistical models. In the 1997 election, Magaloni (1998:231) low educational levels were positive predictors of PRI voter choice in her first model but not her second model. Nevertheless, she hypothesizes that older age—another sociodemographic variable—is one reason for the shift as the older generations start to dealign to either of the opposition alternatives.

16. Poiré (1998:38) found that poverty (as measured by minimum family income) was a positive, statistically significant predictor of PRD and PRI voter choice in the 1994 presidential election. While he did not find educational status to be a statistically significant predictor of PAN, PRI or PRD voter choice in the 1994 presidential election, Poiré (1998:37) only measures postelementary education; that is to say, only those with secondary education. My results consistently demonstrate that it is low educational status (no education or only elementary level education) that explains PRI and PRD voter choice. Thus, the only real difference with respect to the "development complex" sociodemographic factors (income, urban, education) between my results and Poiré's (1998) findings relate to explanations of PAN voter choice in 1994. My findings in 1994 do not measure the presidential election but rather the Morelos 1994 gubernatorial election. In that election, income and urban status are positive statistical predictors of PAN vote choice while education is not as I show above in Table 2.1. The "development complex" thesis has demonstrated that income, urban status and education are so closely associated as to constitute a single explanatory factor (Lipset 1959: 80).

17. This point is illuminated most clearly in the 1997 elections in the states of Colima and Queretaro. In the 1997 Colima election, the mass anti-neoliberal poor vote went to the Workers' Party (PT) ($n = 824$) rather than to the center-left PRD ($n = 131$). The PT historically has been ideologically committed to Marxist-Leninist principles of class struggle. Yet its status as a party independent of the party-state government was ambiguous in the early 1990s (*Proceso* 1999).

18. I split the sample into high-/low-education status subsamples and reran the logit regressions on each of the three political parties to test for the independent effect of education. The only statistically significant results were consistent with the findings on the effects of economic factors discussed in Table 2.1 in relation to poor voters on the left. The evaluation of neoliberal policies was translated into party support in opposite ways: PRI poor uneducated voters viewed their effects positively, while PRD poor uneducated voters viewed the effects negatively.

19. Real wages in Mexico declined by about 50 percent between 1982 and 1988; the real minimum wage declined by 6.1 percent annually between 1988 and 1992 (Samstead and Collier 1995:15). The real purchasing power of salaries also had decreased, by 1998, to a level 60 percent below the level in 1965 *(Informe Presidential* 1998; *La Jornada* 1998).

20. Although the percentages of the labor force occupied in the primary, secondary, and tertiary economic sectors vary by state, the average proportions are 27.1 percent in the primary sector; 24.5 percent in the secondary sector; and 48.3 percent in the tertiary sector (INEGI 1995).

21. The Spanish opposition coalition agreed on the demand for authentic and free elections, legalization of political parties, free unions, free exercise of civil liberties, measures to ensure the jurisdictional autonomy and independence of the judiciary, complete amnesty for political prisoners, return of political exiles, and autonomy for regional minorities ("Una casa" 1976).

22. As noted earlier, this potential unification does not imply the attainment of a "working-class-middle-class" democratizing social coalition (Rueschmeyer et al. 1992) because PRD supporters do not constitute the formal working class as defined by theories of transformative industrialization; and many PAN supporters are members of the "upper classes" or those individuals with the highest levels of education and wealth (see endnote 10).

23. Robert Dahl's (1989:221) well accepted definition of a "polyarchy" with its seven attributes: (1) elected officials, (2) free and fair elections, (3) inclusive suffrage, (4) the right to run for office, (5) freedom of expression, (6) alternative information and (7) associational autonomy is subsumed in my definition.

Chapter 3

Institutional Sources of Delay in Mexico's Transition to Democracy: The Incremental Rise of Judicial Review and Legislative Autonomy (1994–97)

Current theories of the breakdown of authoritarian rule do not mention the role of supreme courts in the democratization process (O'Donnell and Schmitter 1986; Di Palma 1990; Gunther and Higley 1992; Diamond et al. 1989; Lipset 1994). In the literature on this breakdown, constitutional courts are treated as an adjunct to executive power and hence as relatively unimportant to the process of democratization. One exception to this general trend is Huntington (1991:228–231), who comments on the importance of rapid, formal justice by courts in prosecuting officials who violated human rights during the authoritarian phase of the regime. Nevertheless, Huntington (1991:228) assumes that courts have no functional independence from the executive and that justice is "a function of political power."

In this chapter, I show how the incremental rise of judicial review delays a broader separation of powers, a central aspect of democratization in Mexico, with empirical reference to the 1994 judicial reforms in Mexico. These reforms resulted in a slow increase in the Mexican Supreme Court's powers of judicial review of legislation during the breakdown of authoritarian rule (1994–96) but also one subject to retreat and delay. My central hypothesis is that supreme courts' promulgation and exercise of expanded abstract powers of judicial review of legislation will be used both by reformist authoritarian politicians and by democratizing groups, respectively, (1) to increase the perception of democratic legitimacy for an authoritarian regime in crisis and (2) as an anti-authoritarian strategy in the effort to effect the legal leveling of authoritarian political elites to the rule of law (Weber 1978:813).

The democratizing effort to promote abstract justice through greater judicial review of legislation by supreme courts must be understood as a slow rationalizing effort riddled with the tension between formal and substantive rationality (Weber,

1978:641–895). Delay in the fuller separation of powers is the result of the failure of the punitive consequences of legal formalism to be implemented.

In my empirical analysis I demonstrate the incremental trend in the slow rise of the separation of powers from a Mexican Supreme Court with no generalizable powers of judicial review (before December 1994) to a Mexican Supreme Court with the power to generalize the effects of its powers of judicial review (after December 1994). I contend that the events of these initial two years are sufficient to show a slow, halting trend toward formal rationalization and to demonstrate the tension-ridden nature of this process. Indeed, I argue that the earliest years of a supreme court's shift to generalizable powers of the judicial review of legislation show most clearly the strongest struggles over the scope and reach of its new powers. I use the Mexican Supreme Court's expanded powers of judicial review to illustrate the general point that the democratizing press toward formal justice often remains curtailed at the level of its punitive consequences.

THE COMPARATIVE STUDY OF JUDICIAL POLITICS: A NEGLECT OF HISPANIC CONTEXTS

This chapter adds to recent work by scholars in the comparative study of judiciaries, who have addressed the subject of constitutional courts in authoritarian regimes (Tate and Haynie 1993:710; Tate 1987, 1993; Verner 1984).[1] As observed by Tate (1993:74) and by Tate and Haynie (1993:710), the issue of courts in authoritarian regimes is discussed too little, partly because the literature focuses heavily on the courts' independence without analyzing how this autonomy emerged historically. In literature written from the perspective of the totalitarian model of Soviet-led societies, courts are portrayed as politicized extensions of the executive administration, charged with implementing their ideological or political directives (Friedrich and Brezenski Zbigniew 1956:35, 146–47, 186–87, 299). In more highly differentiated scholarly portrayals of courts, the authors have observed that the judiciary might be left with a degree of independence as long as politically sensitive cases were left untouched (Finer 1956:845; Dragnich 1971:410–11) or were shifted to special (often military) courts, as in authoritarian Spain (Linz 1975; Toharia 1974).

Tate and Haynie (1993) showed how authoritarian executive elites ensured the severe reduction of the Philippine Supreme Court's powers of constitutional judicial review of law in the rise of authoritarian rule. Their analysis demonstrates how Philippine authoritarian executive elites strongly curtailed the Supreme Court's existing powers of judicial review in the following areas: (1) reviewing human rights cases, (2) ruling on issues of the separation of powers, (3) ruling on the degree of legitimate executive use of emergency police powers, (4) reviewing executive censorship of the media, (5) reviewing the legality and legitimacy of elections, and (6) reviewing the executive's ability to suspend habeas corpus provisions. The curtailed Supreme Court's extended powers of judicial review were reduced to the sole power of administrative review and to routine supervisory activities of the judiciary and legal system (Tate and Haynie 1993:717, 733–36). These studies help to clarify how executive elites attempting to consolidate authoritarian power will reduce constitutional courts' activities or close them down altogether, as in the case of Fujimori (Peru) and Yeltsin (Russia), when they find them too independent and potentially troublesome (Gillman 1994:368).

I examine the reverse side of this question: the role of the supreme court in the breakdown of authoritarian rule. Using data from the Mexican case, I demonstrate the gradual increase in the Mexican Supreme Court's powers of judicial review into new areas of constitutional law, including the review of human rights violations by political elites, the review of elections and the legitimacy of electoral processes, and the review of the use of emergency military powers by the executive. According to Weber (1978:813), anti-authoritarian democratizing groups attempt to break down authoritarian elites' arbitrary, personalized power by promoting equality before the law. The abstract, universal quality of formal justice constitutes its decisive merit for those democratizing actors who wish to reduce executive arbitrariness and legally to level authoritarian elites to the rule of law. In the Mexican case, democratizing actors also press for abstract formal justice. As I demonstrate, however, the democratizing press toward formal justice often remains curtailed at the level of its punitive consequences.

In this chapter I focus on the rise of judicial review and on an increase in judges' expansive powers, as do sociologies of law in Anglo-American contexts (Wolfe 1986; Morgan and Dwyer 1946). Nevertheless, because of the Latin American judge's role as an interpreter of statutes in keeping with the Napoleonic legal tradition, rather than as an interpreter of precedent, as in the common-law tradition, my analysis falls within the sociologies of law of Hispanic polities (Abel 1988; Toharia 1974; Verner 1984). Thus I attempt to contribute to the growing literature in the sociology of law that focuses on areas outside the common-law world (Abel 1988:1; Abel and Lewis 1995:282; Alba 1969).

THE SUPREME COURT'S ROLE IN DEMOCRATIZING STRUGGLES

The Tension between Formal and Substantive Approaches to Justice

The effort to promote formal equality before the law, an activity associated with the democratizing process not analyzed here, is subject to the contradiction between formal and substantive approaches to justice (Alexander 1983; Beirne 1979; Bendix 1962; Brubaker 1984; Cain 1981; Collins 1988; Dulce 1989; Ewing 1987; Factor and Turner 1994; Feldman 1991; Freund 1968; Habermas 1971; Huff 1989; Hunt 1978; Loewith 1970; Marcuse 1968; Rheinstein 1954; Schlucter 1981; Trieber 1981; Trubek 1972, 1985, 1986; Weber 1978; Zabludovsky 1984, 1986). Some of the themes regarding legal decision-making from the Weberian idiom help to clarify this process. In the Weberian schema of legal decision-making, an abstract formal approach to justice involves an increase in the generality of law and thus increases its abstract calculability. An abstract formal approach to justice "is found where the legally relevant characteristics of the facts are disclosed through the logical analysis of meaning and where, accordingly, definitely fixed legal concepts in the form of highly abstract rules are formulated and applied" (Weber 1978:657). A substantively irrational or informal approach occurs when legal decision making is influenced by particular, often arbitrary features unique to the particular case.[2] Weber contended that the tension between formal and substantive approaches to legal decision-making was endemic because the two were constantly opposed in an "insoluble conflict" (1978:893).

I contend that authoritarian executive elites have no overarching, coherent system of political values in the Weberian sense of ultimate ethical values; rather, political expediency predominates. Indeed, this very commitment to maintaining political power renders authoritarian decision-making on legal matters substantively irrational (empirical) because such decision-making is primarily informal and is conducted case by case. In Mexico, a case-by-case approach to law by authoritarian political elites is the result when legal decisions are made and supreme court rulings are enforced on the basis of arbitrary extralegal factors. The Weberian category of substantive irrationality aptly illuminates this dimension of legal decision-making in authoritarian regimes.

Reducing "Constitutional Gaps" as a Democratizing Strategy: A Sociological Approach

A second issue relevant to this analysis concerns democratizing elites' anti-authoritarian strategies to reduce authoritarian political elites' arbitrary powers over law by expanding the exercise of supreme court powers of constitutional review. In the Weberian mode, legal "gaps" and unregulated areas of the constitution can be understood sociologically as the result of stronger powers' desire to keep control of that arena of social interaction. As Weber contended,

If we understand "constitution" in the sociological sense, as the "modus of distribution of power which determines the possibility of regulating social action", we may indeed, venture the proposition that any community's constitution *in the sociological sense* is determined by the fact of where and how its constitution *in the juridical sense* contains such "gaps," especially with respect to basic questions. Such gaps have been left intentionally where a constitution was rationally enacted by consensus or imposition. This was done simply because the interested party or parties who exercised the decisive influence on the drafting of the constitution in question expected that he or they would ultimately have sufficient power to control, in accordance with their own desires, that portion of social action which, while lacking a basis in any enacted norm, yet had to be carried out somehow. Returning to our illustration: they expected to govern without a budget. (1978:330) (Emphasis added)

In sociological terms, "gaps" in the constitution reflect the continued strength of substantive informal justice over formal justice.

Next I show how insoluble tensions between substantively irrational and formally rational approaches to constitutional justice illustrate the Mexican Supreme Court's transition from limited powers of review of legislation to expanded powers of constitutional review. In the Mexican case, democratizing actors attempt to fill juridical "gaps" in constitutional law regarding basic questions of electoral-political rights. In the sociological sense, this process represents an effort by democratizing opposition parties to shift power toward their constituencies' interests by means of formal law aimed at reducing the executive powers' juridic discretion over constitutional law.

THE 1994 MEXICAN JUDICIAL REFORMS: INCREASING THE PERCEPTION OF DEMOCRATIC LEGITIMATION FOR AN AUTHORITARIAN REGIME IN CRISES

Incoming Mexican President Ernesto Zedillo, proclaiming his commitment to the "rule of law," initiated a series of judicial reforms[3] as a unified package of major constitutional and statutory changes in the jurisdiction and administration of the Mexican federal judiciary (*Diario Oficial de la Federacion*, December 31, 1994). These reforms involved the continued use of the amendment process, following a tradition in Mexican constitutional reforms that had existed since the 1917 constitutional convention.[4] The December 1994 reforms consisted of 27 amendments to substantive constitutional articles and 12 amendments to transitive articles (Melgar Adalid, 1995:15). They included substantial substantive changes to the Supreme Court's functioning and to its expanded powers of the judicial review of legislation. These changes included (1) reducing the number of Supreme Court judges from 24 to 11; (2) changing the terms of Supreme Court justices from six-year periods that coincided with the six-year presidential term to fixed 15-year terms; (3) creating a seven-member Federal Judicial Council to remove some of the administrative burdens on the Supreme Court, including the selection of lower-court judicial candidates and better policing of judicial corruption; (4) increasing the judicial power by explicitly granting the Supreme Court the ability to declare acts of Congress and other federal actions unconstitutional, thereby expanding the Court's sharply restricted constitutional review of laws that previously had lacked precedential value; (5) increasing, from a majority to two-thirds of the Senate, the number of senators necessary to confirm the appointment of Supreme Court nominees; and (6) articulating clearer requirements for nominees to the Court, including not having served as a cabinet minister, administrative agency head, legislator, or governor within a year preceding the nomination.

The overall political-legal context in which Zedillo promulgated the 1994 judicial reforms is critical to understanding their role in increasing the perception of democratic legitimacy for the Mexican regime. Political actors in Mexico take their cases to the Mexican president as a result of the postrevolutionary linkage of party and state historically; no autonomous judiciary exists in Mexico (Garrido

1989:417–34). Informal justice emanating from the centralized office of the president is the law of last recourse. Because the president is the nation's leader as well as the head of the dominant political party, this situation creates the serious legal problem known in Roman law as *Judex non potest esse testis in propria causa* (A judge cannot be a witness in his own cause): The authority is judge and party at the same time (Oropeza 1995:14).

In this legally anomalous context, both before and after the August 1994 presidential elections, most of the major political actors in Mexico complained about the instability and insecurity resulting from what they perceived as the lack of legal guarantees for their various rights. They sought an approximation of the rule of law and an end to arbitrary, informal justice on the part of the Mexican executive. Since the 1970s, for example, opposition political parties in Mexico had protested to the Mexican president about PRI officials' continued fraud, political violence, and arbitrariness in electoral outcomes at the municipal, state, and federal levels. Opposition political parties thus have sought a source of impartial law to ensure unbiased adjudication of electoral outcomes.[5] Similarly, human rights organizations have pressed the president for a "state of law" in Mexico, where an autonomous judiciary would ensure the punishment of state officials who violate citizens' civil and individual rights.[6]

Entrepreneurs have sought to ensure greater constitutional-legal guarantees for property rights. The North American Free Trade Agreement (NAFTA) (1993) legally assured international entrepreneurs that they would be "adequately, effectively and promptly compensated" in the case of expropriation and would be given "access to arbitration for the settlement of disputes" (Stanford 1995:440). Members of domestic private-sector organizations, seeking to stabilize the fiscal system, proposed to the executive eight principal reforms, most notably "juridic security" (defined as respect for "constitutional-legality") and a reduction in discretionary authority by the PRI-dominated Congress and by fiscal administrators (*Proceso* 1996:8). Even a new generation of labor leaders have begun to state the importance of constitutional guarantees for labor and union contractual agreements (*La Jornada* 1996).

Finally, the U.S. government exercised indirect pressure on Mexico in 1994 to stabilize its political system because of concern about the financial market and the crisis-like political climate resulting from a series of high-level political assassinations. During that year the PRI presidential candidate and the party's attorney general were assassinated; in addition, prominent businessmen were kidnapped, and a protracted armed rebellion occurred in the southern state of Chiapas (*The Economist* 1995:36–37; DePalma 1995:E3).

In other words, the December 1994 judicial reforms did not emerge in a political vacuum. Rather, they involved a multifaceted attempt to increase the perception of democratic legitimacy for an authoritarian regime in crisis. The multiple aspects of the 1994 judicial reforms are evident in the fact that they appeal to, or appease, each of the PRI's major supporters and opponents. In appealing to middle-class electors' demands for greater juridic security and legal certainty, Zedillo announced the preparation of the 1994 judicial reforms in a campaign speech in Guadalajara, one of Mexico's most middle-class cities and a stronghold of the PAN, the rightist oppositional, pro-business political party.[7] The 1994 judicial reforms also appeased the opposition political parties' demand for greater political influence by legitimating their ability to bring forward laws for constitutional review.[8] Finally, Zedillo's 1994 judicial reforms enabled the U.S. administration to claim that "Ernesto Zedillo is serious about promoting the rule of law."[9]

INCREASING THE ABSTRACT POWER OF LAW: EXPANDING THE COURT'S POWERS OF JUDICIAL REVIEW

Although comparative studies of judicial systems commonly use terms adopted from liberal theory, such as *judicial review*, we find wide variation in nations' distinctive histories and in the extent to which executive elites are willing to assault the judiciary's independence and impartiality (Tate 1993; Gillman 1994:373; Von Lazar 1971). In Mexico, before the 1994 judicial reforms, the Mexican Supreme Court possessed severely limited power to review acts of the other branches of government. The Court's constitutional review of laws also was sharply restricted; that is, it had no generalizable power of abstract review. Instead, since the 1850s the Supreme Court has possessed powers of limited judicial review through the writ of *amparo* (Burgoa 1951; Carpizo 1978:178–181; Padgett 1976; Ramirez 1994; Scott 1964). Under this writ, the Court may issue a stay of government action if it finds that implementation of the action may violate the rights or interests of an individual or a group (Verner 1984:472). The court's historical power to employ this writ has enabled it to protect individuals against violations of their rights by state authorities (Fix-Zamudio and Cossio Diaz 1995). Thus the effective use of judicial review is directly related to the independence of the judiciary in Latin America (Padgett 1976:201–5).

Yet the Mexican Supreme Court's writ of *amparo* has been sharply restricted by the Court's ability to declare a law unconstitutional only in regard to the individual in question (Garcia 1981:342). The inability to set legal precedent through the constitutional review of law has severely limited the Supreme Court's power in relation to that of the executive branch. Accordingly the 1994 judicial reforms must be understood in terms of the institutional design of the Mexican legal system. In 1824, in its first constitution, Mexico copied the U.S. system of separation of powers and of powers of judicial review. In theory, when the Supreme Court declares a law unconstitutional, the restrictions on the generalizability of such a declaration function adequately in U.S. juridical culture because the lesser courts respect the Supreme Court's decisions and because every citizen has the right to bring up a matter for constitutional review. In Mexico, however, according to one prominent Mexican legal scholar and admirer of the U.S. Supreme Court, the problem with the history of judicial ideas is that "Mexico copied the U.S. in its 1824 Constitution but we have little respect for the Supreme Court and Mexican citizens cannot challenge the general constitutionality of a law" (Institute for Juridic Studies 1995).

Gonzalez Casanova (1965), in his study of democracy in Mexico, used the total number of times the Mexican Supreme Court conceded to the executive branch a writ of *amparo* between 1917 and 1960 as an index of the Court's autonomy in relation to the executive. He found that the court issued a writ of *amparo* in favor of the executive on 1,042 occasions, or 66% of the time, and negated the executive's demands on 521 occasions, or 34% of the time (Gonzalez Casanova 1965:237). Nevertheless, this study shows that most of the Court's opposition periods were historically specific: They were limited to the immediate postrevolutionary period during the presidencies of Carranza and Huerta, or to opposition to the expropria- tion of property during the revolution's consolidation phase in the Cardenas era. The court's writ of *amparo* had no precedential value in any of these cases. In Weberian terms, the curtailment of judicial review illustrates the limited strength of abstract formal justice and the greater strength of informal, case-by-case justice.

The 1994 judicial reforms granted to the Mexican Supreme Court, for the first time, the ability to set precedent by explicitly extending the reach of its abstract powers; thus the Court was enabled to declare acts of Congress and other federal actions unconstitutional. In theory, the increased powers of judicial review and the power to review legislation could further the representative system and could increase political minorities' participation in Congress by protecting them from abuses of PRI majoritarianism (*Harvard Law Review* 1995). A stronger Supreme Court might also reduce PRI-controlled presidential power and allow for a corre- lated expansion of congressional power. In the long run, expanded judicial review might increase meaningful separation of powers with judicially monitored democ- racy. Thus, in addition to the actual structural changes caused by the 1994 judicial reforms, the major potential change is the extension of the generalizability or the abstract reach of the Court's powers of constitutional review. The brief Mexican experience with expanded judicial review (1994–96) allows us to study the institu- tional consequences of the attempt to impose democratization from "above" through the rule of law, in a situation in which the Supreme Court historically has been subordinate to the executive.

DATA SOURCES

The cases cited here are drawn from the Mexican Supreme Court registrar. Data on the political consequences of the legal cases are taken from the major opposition newspapers and weekly journals from March 1995 to December 1996. My sample is fully representative of all cases of constitutional judicial review during this period.

RESULTS AND DISCUSSION: THE COURT'S RULINGS (1994–96)

The move toward greater judicial review is illustrated by the Supreme Court's response and by its adherence to abstract formalism in its responses to new cases brought forward for constitutional review in the period after December 1994 (1994–96).

Strict Legal-Formalism: Legally Channeling the Political Opposition and Upholding Constitutional Validity

As Table 3.1 suggests, the 1994 reforms gave the political opposition an opportunity to bring laws forward for abstract constitutional review, as evidenced in the variety of new cases before the Court. These cases concerned, for example, the sales tax, investigations of human rights violations, violations of election spending limitations, and violations of political rights of representation. At the same time, government officials also could take advantage of the new freedom to bring laws forward for constitutional review: For example, the governor of Tabasco sought to challenge the attorney general's legal ability to investigate his alleged campaign spending violations.

The movement toward greater "rule of law" and greater abstract powers of judicial review is also evident in the Court's strict adherence to legal formalism as the basis for rejecting various social groups' demands for the constitutional review of laws. In the December 1994–96 period, the Court unanimously rejected any efforts by actors such as nongovernmental organizations or law professors to bring forward cases for constitutional review on the legal-formal grounds that the 1994 judicial reforms allowed only government officials and a quorum of 33 percent of the political parties in the legislature to bring a case forward for review (see Table 3.1). The court also rejected the demand of various Mexican human rights organizations and their legal advisors that it act as an ombudsman to investigate violations of human rights by members of the state police (*La Jornada* June 26, 1995). This point is illustrated in the case of the June 1995 massacre of 17 peasants in the village of Aguas Blancas, Guerrero.

The Supreme Court's response in the Aguas Blancas case was to agree with the social transcendence of the issue and to observe that the Court cannot remain "indifferent before events such as these, given its historical responsibility [and the fact that] its function is fundamentally the protection of individual guarantees" (*La Jornada* October 3, 1995). All of the justices agreed, however, that the coalition of 145 Mexican human rights organizations lacked the "active legitimacy" to ask for the court's intervention because Constitutional Article 97 states explicitly that the petition for the Court to investigate violations of individual rights must come directly from the president, state governors, or Congress (*La Jornada* October 3, 1995).

Table 3.1
Impact of 1994 Judicial Reforms: Experimentation in Judicial Review by Political Opposition; Supreme Court Rulings on the Constitutionality of Laws, 1994–96

Type of law brought forward for constitutional review by 33 % of the legislature.	Cases have no legal standing because of Supermajority Requirement (8/11).	Cases have no legal standing because of lack of Court's jurisdiction or other technical grounds. Extraordinary faculties of Court to review violations of constitutional rights
Increase in Sales Tax, May 1995.	Rejected, 6/5.	
Law Professors challenge president' use of military in Chiapas on grounds that a state of emergency not previously declared, August 1995.		Rejected. Only President, governors, or 33 percent of Congress can legitimately petition Court to serve as ombudsman.
Tabasco state governor's constitutional challenge to authority of attorney general office's to investigate campaign-spending violations, Sept. 1995.		Rejected. Attorney General has legal jurisdiction to investigate and prosecute electoral crimes.
Mexican Human Rights Commission demand Supreme Court investigate violations of individual human rights resulting from Aguas Blancas Peasant Massacre, October 1995.		Rejected. Only president, governors, or 33 % of Congress can legitimately petition Court to hear cases for constitutional review.
Opposition political parties' constitutional challenge to PRI's new non-party Federal District Citizen's Counselors on grounds that it violates political rights to representation through political parties, November 1995.	Rejected, 6/5. Majority upholds Court's self-restraint and exclusion of electoral rights from constitutional review.	
Opposition political parties challenge president's use of military in Chiapas on grounds that a state of emergency not previously declared, January 1996.		Rejected, 11/0. In cases of grave perturbation to public peace or grave danger to society, military can act outside the barracks as long as they subordinate themselves to the juridic and civil order, do not suspend and scrupulously respect individual rights.
President requests Court to appoint ombudsman to investigate human rights violations in Aguas Blancas peasant massacre, April 1996.		Court issues moral statement condemning state governor as responsible for violating human rights, covering up the truth found in previous investigations, deceiving the public and obstructing justice by manipulating the Aguas Blancas investigation. Extraordinary power.
Opposition political parties challenge recent PRI-based electoral reforms denying the Congress the ability to make decisions regarding the electoral process on the basis of "abstract, general and impersonal" norms, November 1996.		Federal Electoral Code valid in allowing federal electoral administration to decide amount of public campaign financing per party as long as it is "subject to law."

Sources: *La Jornada* March 31, 1995 (sales tax); *La Jornada* August 4, 1995 (Chiapas); *Reforma* August 21, 1995: 5A; *Proseco* 985, September 18, 1995: 16–20 (campaign spending violations); *La Jornada* July 26, 1995 (Aguas Blancas); August 11, 1995; August 12, 1995; October 3, 1995: March 8, 1996 (Aguas Blancas); *La Jornada* November 11, 1995 (D.F. Citizens' Counselors); Semanario Judicial de la Federacio y Su Gaceta, Novena Epoco, Tomo III, March 1996: 434–37; *Proceso* 1009, March 4, 1996: 8–11; 1016, April 22, 1996: 16–22; 1017, April 29, 1996: 6–13 (Aguas Blancas); 1049, December 8 1995: 9; *La Jornada* January 8, 1997: 2 (campaign spending limits and Congress).

Similarly, the Supreme Court rejected claims by UNAM and UAM law professors Javier Garrido, Emilio Krieger, Agustin Perez Carrillo, and Alejandro del Palacio that the presence of the Mexican Army in Chiapas was unconstitutional on the grounds that it was dislocating individuals, violating security, and superseding multiple local and federal laws without the previous declaration of a state of emergency (*La Jornada* August 4, 1995). The professors exhorted the Court to be "the juridic conscience of the nation and the ultimate instance of the state of law," especially in view of the serious violations of the Constitution, including violations to domestic security and the blocking of public access ways (*La Jornada* August 4, 1995). In their petition, they reminded the Court that their request for intervention by the Court before the December 1994 reforms had been simply ignored. They stated that what was needed was a change in attitude, a true division of powers, and the Court's fulfillment of its role in standing up for the constitutional order (*La Jornada* August 4 1995).

The court heard the Chiapas case, however, after it was brought forward by 33 percent of the legislature. It upheld the "constitutional validity" of those constitutional articles under the National System of Public Security, which permits the army to move in cases of grave disturbance of public peace (Semanario Judicial 1996:435). Nevertheless, the Court also issued a statement of the clear limitations on the use of the military for threats to public security, stating that guaranteed rights should not be threatened and that such usage should not extend beyond the limited reach legally guaranteed (Semanario Judicial 1996:435).

This group of rulings shows that the Supreme Court adhered to strict legal formalism in matters of procedure. As a result, the various nonparliamentary democratic opposition movements were restricted in their ability to bring forward cases for judicial review.[10] In fact, in both the nongovernmental human rights organizations' attempt to bring up the Aguas Blancas peasant massacre for judicial review and the law professors' attempt to bring up the question of executive use of military force without a declaration of a state of emergency, actors in civil society were forced to comply with legal formal procedure and to channel their demands into law-bound forums. Moreover, legal formalism was justified on the grounds that the validity of existing constitutional articles must be upheld.

Strict Legal-Formalism: Ruling against the Regime

The Supreme Court adhered to a strictly formal interpretation of the 1994 reforms in declaring the case of the PRI governor of Tabasco "not precedential" on the grounds that the attorney general (headed by a member of PAN, the rightist opposition party) had the legal authority to investigate and prosecute state governors' electoral crimes (*Reforma* 1995:5; *Proceso* 1995:16–20). In this case, legal formalism worked politically in a direction opposite to the above cases to facilitate the investigation of a PRI state governor's alleged electoral misdeeds, against his wishes and the wishes of 33 percent of his PRI-dominated Tabasco legislature.

This was also the political implication of the Supreme Court's response to Zedillo's historically unprecedented request that it employ its extraordinary powers under Article 97 and act as an impartial ombudsman to investigate human rights violations in the massacre of 17 peasants by state police in Aguas Blancas. After investigating the case, the Court issued a strong statement condemning the Guerrero state governor as responsible for violating human rights in the peasants' death, of covering up the truth found in previous investigations, of deceiving the public, and of obstructing justice by manipulating the Aguas Blancas investigation.[11]

In both the Tabasco and the Aguas Blancas cases, the Supreme Court's adherence to strict legal formalism worked politically against the PRI party-state. These cases challenge the idea that courts in authoritarian regimes lack the autonomy to rule on politically sensitive matters whose consequences oppose the ruling party-state's interests. Rather, they suggest an unevenness and an internal contradiction in the Mexican democratizing transition between the legal system and the political system of authority. Although issued at an early point in the reform, these rulings against the regime suggest that formal justice implemented in authoritarian contexts has consequences undesirable to the political group in power.

Strict Legal Formalism and Fear: Restricting the Court's Expanded Powers of Judicial Review

Nevertheless, in the most sensitive areas of expanded judicial review—elections, electoral legitimacy, and the executive's use of emergency powers—strict legal formalism restrained the Supreme Court from greater assertiveness. In an effort to reduce possible further expansion of the Court's new powers of judicial review, Zedillo's 1994 judicial reforms required agreement by a "supermajority" of Supreme Court ministers (eight of 11), rather than a simple majority (six of 11), for a law to be considered unconstitutional (*Diario Oficial de la Federacion*, December 31, 1994). At the initiation of the reforms in December 1994, constitutional legal scholars criticized this "supermajority" provision; they argued that the number was too high and predicted that the provision would stymie the court (Fix-Fierro 1995:173–78).

Indeed, this concern by legal theorists proved prophetic: The Supreme Court was divided on its rulings in the case of the federal district elections citizens' election for councilor. The immediate legal issue was whether the ruling party could exclude the opposition parties from competing for the new position of municipal federal district councilor (*consejero ciudadano*). The PRI had banned the opposition parties from running candidates, and demanded instead that candidates run as private "citizens." The political opposition immediately challenged the constitutionality of the new federal district citizens' councilor law on the grounds that it denied citizens their constitutional political rights; Constitutional Article 41 considers political parties as entities in the public interest (*Proceso* 984, 1995:10). Therefore political parties have the right to participate in the nation's democratic life and in the selection of national representatives.

The basic constitutional issue was whether the court should reconfirm its historical self-restraint in not ruling on issues of elections, electoral legitimacy, and electoral fraud. This self-restraint in matters of elections has its historical precedent in an 1882 decision by Chief Justice Ignacio Vallarta, who contended that the Court "is incompetent in origin—that it shall not intervene to solve political questions that correspond, by constitutional disposition, to other branches of government" (*Jurisprudencia* 1985:272: Oropeza 1995:13). This self-restraint may have enabled the Court's other powers to remain functional during long periods of one-party dictatorships, when it was widely feared that the institution would be dissolved altogether by the executive powers (Barragán 1994). Today, however, legal theorists advocate overturning the Court's self-restraint. Arturo Zaldivar, the founding member of the Mexican Academy of Constitutional and Amparo (Habeas Corpus) Law of the Mexican Bar, commented as follows with respect to the December 1994 judicial reforms:

it is contradictory that we talk about having a Constitutional Tribunal above the Supreme Court but at the same time, we take away from it the power of the constitutional review of electoral material. The world-wide trend is that constitutional tribunals analyze these type of problems irrespective of the types of material, even electoral material. This does not mean [that] the Court should convert itself into a Federal Electoral Tribunal, one of these already exists, but rather electoral laws should be subject to constitutional control. For example, were it the case that one of the Federal Code of Institutions and Electoral Procedures (COFIPE) were unconstitutional, "you cannot do anything. There is no way to impugn it. What are we doing? Elevating the ordinary legislator to the status of a Constituent Power because that law cannot be rejected. We [Mexicans] have to rid ourselves of the fear that the Court review electoral questions as constitutional issues." (*Proceso* 946, 1994:35)

As shown in Table 3.1, in the Supreme Court's November 1, 1995 decision, a simple majority of justices (six of 11) agreed that electoral material should be subject to constitutional review and that the Court should set a defined criterion as to what constitutes "electoral material" (*Proceso* 992, 1996:35). This was especially necessary, argued the majority, in light of the fact that the 1917 constitution had not established a "defense mechanism" for citizens' political rights in the case of a law's supposed unconstitutionality (*La Jornada* November 1, 1995:1). All electoral law should fall under the jurisdiction of the Supreme Court, said the majority. A minority of five justices, however, including the two holdover justices from the previous Supreme Court, argued that the issue of the federal district citizens' councilor lacked jurisdictional character because it was an electoral issue. In addition, they argued, citizens' councils are organs of public power established by an election; thus they have an electoral character (*La Jornada* November 1, 1995:1). Hence, as legal theorists foresaw, the "supermajority" provision written into the December 1994 judicial reforms functioned conservatively to prevent the subordination of electoral law to constitutional review.

In this case, because of adherence to strict legal formalism, the minority opinion (five of 11 justices) prevailed: The court should continue not to engage in reviewing elections or electoral legitimacy. Supreme Court Minister Juventino Castro y Castro justified the Court's continued self-restraint and its refusal to act as a constitutional arbitrator by invoking an old historical fear that resurfaced in the October-November 1995 debates on the Court's role of reviewing electoral laws. Minister Castro y Castro argued as follows:

A Court which has no army, that doesn't control the budget, and that doesn't manage foreign relations, could only with great difficulty put itself over the other two powers. Everything is in the hands of the Executive, and the moment that the Court might want to put itself above the other two powers, very simply and easily the president, who is the natural head of the Army, would simply do away with the Court. (*Proceso* 992, November 6, 1995: 36)

The continued fear of Supreme Court involvement in electoral justice and the associated idea that the Court should dedicate itself solely to juridical matters, so as not to become involved, contaminated, or drawn into the political order and party politics, also allow the executive continued unchecked power in electoral law.

This fear is also expressed in the Supreme Court's decision, in the Chiapas case, to reaffirm the executive's power to move the army out of barracks to keep domestic peace without a previous declaration of emergency. Further, this fear indirectly upholds presidential power because the Court partly justified its legal reasoning in the Chiapas case on the basis of laws promulgated under the National System of Public Security. This administrative organ, which the previous Mexican president created by decree in 1994, gives the president unchecked power to use security forces to ensure public order in situations of threats to national security (Krieger 1994:295).

Both of these cases demonstrate how the executive branch can undercut the judiciary's power to hold it accountable; this is a general problem in Latin America (Buscaglia et al. 1995:13). They also support Tate and Haynie's finding that the fear of coercion causes at least some judges to alter their decisions so as to please the ruler in authoritarian regimes (Tate and Haynie 1993:735). The effect of this fear of executive-level coercion is quite evident in the case of ex-Court Minister Mariano Azuela, whom Zedillo dismissed in December 1994 in his overhauling of the Court. When asked whether the December 1994 reforms would end the Supreme Court's tendency to subordinate itself to the executive's wishes, Azuela replied:

I have in my personal experience never received any pressures. I have always acted with absolute independence. [However], I have in some manner the sensation that there was always a latent worry, the fear that in [legal] themes of certain importance (declaring the unconstitutionality of a law, for example), one assumes a contrary attitude, that this could make the executive angry. And in a system in which the Executive does not want anyone to touch it or to limit it, the easiest thing to do is to reform the Constitution, to eliminate life-terms for ministers, and to throw out onto the street all the previous ministers. Of course, were there an independent Senate and Chamber of Deputies, this could not occur. Yet, what is certain is that one knows that not only can it happen but it can easily happen. I attribute this to the fact that there have been some decisions made influenced by this fear, even though

I have no proof to say that is was a designation of the Executive. Rather, more likely, that the majority saw some pronouncement or another as a very grave risk. (*Proceso* 951, 1995:39)

In this statement, Azuela expresses the cautious, fearful criticism of a member of the legal profession who historically has been closely associated with the regime, and demonstrates how fear of executive coercion influences Supreme Court ministers' decisions.

The Political Context: Nullifying the Punitive Consequences of the Court's Legal-Formal Rulings and the Attempt to Continue the Reign of Informal, Case-by-Case Justice

This review of Mexican Supreme Court rulings in the post-1994 judicial reform period shows the tension between abstract, formal justice and the law-transcending, informal justice preferred by members of the bureaucratically articulated group in power. Various social actors such as opposition political parties, law professors, independent business groups, and the Supreme Court itself stand on the side of legal formalism and the rule of law. State governors and many members of the PRI support the continuation of centralized, informal presidential control. The most revealing aspect of the post-1994 judicial reforms, however, is the executive's continued informal power to direct law toward its political ends. This control is most apparent in the effect of the "supermajority" provisions on the Supreme Court's decisions. Had the 1994 judicial reforms granted the Mexican Supreme Court the power to review the constitutionality of laws on the basis of a simple majority rather than a supermajority, the Court's powers of judicial review would have been increased. That the reforms did not do so demonstrates the continued existence of executive-level power embodied in law, and its indirect dominance over the judicial branch.

Indeed, it was a PRI legislative committee that nullified any further legal effects of the Supreme Court's ruling in the Aguas Blancas case by canceling the process of political judgment on Guererro state governor Ruben Figueroa. Such a judgment could have barred him from holding political office for 20 years (*La Jornada* May 31, 1996). PRI legislators agreed that Figueroa committed grave violations of the constitution in the case of Aguas Blancas, but they argued that these were not sufficient or "systematic" enough to require that he submit to judgment. This decision provoked one reporter to ask, "How many deaths does the PRI need so that a violation to the Constitution be considered grave and systematic?" (*La Jornada* May 31, 1996). Less emotionally, the Supreme Court minister in charge of investigating the Aguas Blancas case concluded that the official political reaction to the investigation was "indifference" because neither the president, anyone in the attorney general's office, nor the authorities of the State of Guerrero had requested the complete file on the investigation. They had merely "examined the dictum" to fix their positions and did not demonstrate the least interest in the complete file" (*La Jornada* July 3, 1996).

Similarly, law-transcending decision-making was the basis on which the Tabasco state attorney general's office closed the case of state governor Roberto Madrazo on the grounds that there was no "illicit" use of campaign funds (*La Jornada* July 8, 1996). By Mexican law, the federal attorney general's investigations of electoral crimes are turned over to the local district attorney for prosecution. The state-level legal decision not to prosecute was made in the face of the federal attorney general's report. This report concluded, on the basis of documented evidence, that the Tabasco governor had spent 30 times more money than permitted by state law (*Proceso* 1023, 1996:7). Initially, when the federal attorney general (a member of PAN and the first non-PRI cabinet member in Mexican postrevolutionary history) finished his investigation, Governor Madrazo, a PRI member, argued that the accusations were "false, painful, immoral, and lacking in juridic sense." Madrazo stated that the attorney general acted to "serve a political party over the service of the nation" (*Proceso* 1023, 1996:7). Despite multiple forms of evidence linking the governor to the illicit sources of campaign funds and to vast overspending of funds during his campaign, Zedillo subsequently embraced him in public, a symbol, in Mexican political culture, of continued life (May 1996). The Tabasco state district attorney's decision to close the Madrazo case illustrates the continued role of law-transcending, politically based decisions. In theoretical terms, these decisions are made on the basis of expediency or a case-by-case calculus; that is, they represent informal justice.

Nevertheless, the undermining of legal formalism in the Madrazo case caused significant political repercussions for the regime's legitimacy. Indeed, the whole issue on which the Madrazo case rested—the attempt to prosecute violations of campaign spending limits and to ensure adherence to legal limits—became the principal reason for the 1996 electoral pact. The pact itself was a product of 22 months of elite-level negotiations between the presidency and the main rightist and leftist democratic opposition parties. These negotiations broke down in September 1996: The two democratic opposition parties pulled out of the accords at the last minute, when PRI legislators rewrote the reforms so as to increase campaign spending figures, reduce the amount of media time given to the opposition parties, and increase opposition parties' difficulty in fielding coalition candidates. This action was a political embarrassment for Zedillo because he had personally supported the pact and had promoted it, since January 1995, as a centerpiece of political reform for his administration.

Instead the issue of campaign spending limitations became juridified. Opposition parties brought the issue to the court in a challenge to the November 1996 electoral reforms, which had been passed unilaterally by the PRI. The opposition alleged that the November 1996 reforms granted the federal electoral bureaucracy greater discretion only in deciding campaign spending limits. They argued that precisely on these grounds, the PRI electoral reforms limited congressional power to make judgments about elections on the basis of general, abstract, and impersonal norms (*Proceso* 1049, 1996:9).

Here, too, however, the issue of general norms is bypassed by the Supreme Court's ruling that Article 49 of the Federal Electoral Code grants the federal electoral bureaucracy the right to decide the relative proportion of campaign funds for each party (and thus a greater share of public monies to the PRI) as long as it obeys the law (*La Jornada* January 8, 1997a:1). In the opinion of the Supreme Court, their legal judgment that Article 49 of the Federal Electoral Code was not unconstitutional was "strictly juridical"; it neither "resolved" nor "upheld" any opinion regarding the fairness of campaign financing (*La Jornada* January 8, 1997a:1). As for the normative constitutionality of the issue of campaign financing, the Supreme Court said it would "undertake a study of the general issue" proposed by the opposition parties. Thus the 1997 case involving campaign spending represents yet another anti-authoritarian effort by democratizing groups to promote abstract formal justice. This effort, however, also failed to ensure the legal leveling of the political elite to abstract justice.

ANALYSIS

The 1994–96 court rulings suggest that Zedillo's attempt to move Mexican society toward the "rule of law," to renounce the metaconstitutional powers of the executive, and to promote legal formalism has been curtailed at the level of punitive consequences. The continued existence of law-transcending practices by the bureaucratically articulated group in power (the PRI) has blocked the Court's extension into the constitutional review of elections and electoral practices. In addition, PRI-directed nullifications of accusations of legal wrongdoing, which may be issued indirectly from the Mexican president's office, have effectively blocked any potential legal consequences of decisions made on the basis of legal formalism.

These findings suggest that the democratizing effort to promote abstract justice must be understood developmentally, as a slow, rationalizing effort riddled with the tension between formal and substantive irrationality. A neo-Weberian approach incorporating the dialectics of formal rationality and substantive irrationality allows us to see clearly the nature of this legal-political struggle. The first two years of cases under the Court's new powers of extended judicial review show evidence of a trend toward greater legal formalism. These cases also show a struggle between members of the legal system and members of the political system of rule, in which the latter often prefer the continuation of informal, case-by-case justice. This delays a transition toward the greater separation of powers.

In regard to the actual effects of extended judicial review on the democratizing struggle in Mexico, the empirical results are also mixed. On one hand, the expanded possibilities for formal rationalization of law allow democratizing groups to translate their issues into abstract legal terms for formal conceptual review by the Court. The Court's review of all the major cases—the law professors' challenge to Zedillo's use of the military in Chiapas, the democratizing opposition parties' challenge to

Madrazo's overspending on campaign limits, and to the PRI's attempt to hold "nonparty" federal district citizens' councillor elections, and the request by human rights groups (and later by Zedillo) that the court review the massacre of peasants at Aguas Blancas—all set into motion the Supreme Court justices' general application of universal legal notions to the particular cases at hand.

Slowly, formal equality before the law is promoted by bringing forward these cases, and by the pressure exerted on the Court to rule on them in abstract terms, insofar as normative and political pressures are placed on the Court to set abstract precedent. Even when the Court majority declines to involve itself, as in its review of the constitutionality of the Court's self-restraint in electoral matters, the minority opinion formulates the argument in favor of expanded judicial review—that is, greater abstract judicial power. The promotion of formal abstract universality before the law inadvertently promotes the egalitarian demands of democratizing groups.

On the other hand, the bureaucratically articulated group in power (the PRI) is clearly rejecting the punitive legal consequences of formal equality in a political context dominated by a tradition of informal, material justice. The continuation of informal, material justice on a case-by-case basis is demonstrated by the ruling group's continued bureaucratic power and by its ability to politically impose extralegal justice: In both the Madrazo and the Aguas Blancas cases, PRI-dominated legislatures merely ignored or overturned the Court's rulings. The continuation of justice on the basis of political expediency is anti-democratic in that it effaces the legal leveling implications of democratizing groups' demands; that is, it ignores the democratizing demand that the political elite also be subordinated to the rule of law. This point supports previous findings that authoritarian rulers will simply ignore judges' orders when they do not find them to be in their interests (Tate 1993:319). The continuation of these interests thus delays the construction of institutional structures of the state in which the relative degree of the dispersion of power for the implementation of the punitive consequences of legal-formalist extends more widely beyond individuals associated with the old regime.

IMPLICATIONS

The Mexican case shows the court as a focal point for democratizing struggles in the breakdown of authoritarian rule. In this role, Supreme Court justices are caught between the tasks of extending judicial review into new areas of constitutional law and attempting to avoid entanglement in partisan political conflicts. In such a delicate position, the Court's rulings are used strategically by democratizing groups to legitimate their positions, are employed by the ruling party to legitimate its position, or are ignored by either or both in their partisan struggles. At the same time, these rulings set calculable legal precedent and thus become legally institutionalized, with the implication of relevance for similar democratizing struggles in the future. In this sense, Supreme Court ministers contribute to the longer-term rationalizing effort by increasing the degree of calculability of law and by enlarging democratizing groups' access to the legal system.

Greater formal abstract review of law resulting from the efforts of democratizing groups is occurring in Mexico, even while the official party-state avoids formal equality and its punitive consequences in favor of extralegal, informal justice. The brief Mexican experiment in judicial review (1994–96) in a democratizing context shows that the transition from authoritarian rule is fraught with the tension between formal and informal substantive approaches to justice. The Mexican case also shows that although the Supreme Court may move toward greater legal formalism, its role in pressing for adherence to the abstract, universal principles of law is necessarily limited in the absence of a fully functioning oppositional party system and real alteration of political power. Court rulings based on the principles of abstract formal justice can be undermined by those political actors whose interests are not served best by legal formalism, although such undermining always comes at a cost to the regime's legitimacy.

The main general lesson to be learned here is that courts in fact play a role in democratizing struggles and in the breakdown of authoritarian rule. This finding encourages us to think about that role rather than to ignore it. My evidence suggests that strict adherence to legal formalism can have three consequences: (1) It can channel the political opposition into legal formal arenas and can uphold constitutional validity; (2) it can lead to rulings against the political elite; and (3) it can be used to justify restricting the court from judicial review in sensitive areas of electoral legitimacy and in the executive's use of emergency powers. These findings suggest that intrastate relationships between executive and legal elites are subtle and multifaceted, and must be studied in terms of their nuances. The court plays a central role in attempting to adhere to principles of formal justice in a highly partisan political context.

CODA: THE SLOW RISE OF LEGISLATIVE AUTONOMY

The July 1997 elections inaugurated divided government in Mexico's national legislature for the first time in its history. The distribution of seats in Mexico's lower house or "Chamber of Deputies," gave the political opposition a majority (24.8 percent PAN; 25 percent PRD; 2.8 percent other) and left the PRI without a majority (47.8 percent) of the seats (*Reforma* 1997; MacLeod 1999:2). In the Senate, however, the PRI held onto its majority.

In the post-1997 Mexican legislature, a slow trend toward greater legislative autonomy from centralized executive control is also evident. By mid-1999, the post-1997 LVII Legislature saw a rise in the overall number of laws passed: 123 laws approved in the July 1997 to July 1999 period versus 119 total laws approved in the entire previous legislature (Meyer 1998b). This represents a rise in the sheer amount of legislation of over 50 percent (*Excelsior* 1999a). Moreover, 60 percent of this legislation in the post-1997 period was proposed by legislators versus 40 percent presented by the executive (Miranda 1999). This represents a clear diminution of executive control over the legislature and an increase in its relative autonomy from it (*Excelsior* 1999a).

Moreover, the type of legislation approved by the post-1997 legislature also reveals the slow rise of the legislative action promoting the slow diminution of centralized executive control. The Law to Reform the Mexican Human Rights Commission, Municipal Reform, and Reforms to the Chamber itself (Underwood 1998; Ugalde 1999) effect legal changes designed to eventuate in an increase in the separation of powers. Of course, this process of formal rationalization has not been a linear one: numerous fights, threats, intransigence, unkeep promises, and efforts to paralyze the Chamber have also characterized the post-1997 Mexican legislature (Miranda 1999). Moreover, the punitive consequences of legal formalism are not always implemented, as the earlier analysis in this chapter demonstrates, as well as the difficulties of congressional banking oversight committees to audit alleged illegal bank contributions to the PRI political campaigns suggests (*The News* 1999). Ugalde (1999) also suggests that the legislature initially lacked operating procedures, and infrastructure to properly oversee the executive and that even the creation of the "fiscalization committee" to oversee the spending of tax money in 1998 will not begin in full until the year 2000 (Aguayo 1999).

The back-and-forth nature of both the rise of judicial review and of legislative autonomy is consistent with a development approach to the transition to legal-rational abstract rule, best understood as a slow effort riddled with the tension between formal and substantive approaches to legal decision-making. If the trend toward abstract formal rationality is supported by the executive branch, one should expect that branch to function legally as such. That it sometimes does not suggests the need to examine sociologically the party-state bureaucracy members' intractable power to obstruct legal formalism when its consequences damage their interests. The potential damage of legal formalism for the bureaucratically articulated ruling group allows us to predict, in the case of Mexico, that democratizing groups will continue to use abstract formal justice in a strategic attempt to legally level the authoritarian executive elite to formal equality before the law in their efforts to break down personalized, informal authoritarian power.

NOTES

1. For literature on the study of the institutional performance of courts, see Theodore Becker, *Comparative Judicial Politics* (Chicago: Rand McNally, 1970); Jean Blondel, *An Introduction to Comparative Government* (New York: Praeger 1969); Robert C. Fried, *Comparative Political Institutions*, (New York: Macmillian, 1966); Henry W. Ehrmann, *Comparative Legal Cultures* (Englewood Cliffs, NJ: Prentice-Hall 1976); John R. Schmidhauser, "Alternative Conceptual Frameworks in Comparative Cross-National Legal and Judicial Research," in *Comparative Judicial Systems: Challenging Frontiers in Conceptual and Empirical Analysis.* Advances in Political Science: An International Series, vol. 6 (London: Butterworth, 1987); Martin H. Shapiro, "Courts," in *The Handbook of Political Science,* vol. 5, edited by Fred I. Greenstein and Nelson W. Polsby (Reading, MA: Addison-Wesley 1975), pp. 321–73. *Governmental Institutions and Processes* (Reading, MA: Addison-Wesley 1975).

2. Of course, law-making could also be *formally irrational* "when one applies . . . means which cannot be controlled by the intellect, for instance, when recourse is had to oracles or substitutes therefore" (Weber 1978: 656). Legal decision-making could also be *substantively rational* if the decision of legal problems is influenced by norms different from those obtained through the logical generalization of abstract interpretations of meaning (1978: 657). This refers to the satisfaction of ultimate values or needs, derived from sources such as an internal moral framework, religious faith, or political commitments—but not derived from and indeed unrelated to the rules and principles of the legal system itself.

3. The executive sent the December 1994 judicial reforms to the Mexican Senate on April 18, 1995, for deliberation by various subcommittees (Justice, Governing, Legislative Studies) (*Diario de los Debates*, Senado de la Republica, April 24, 1995: 81). In the subsequent span of eight days, a total of five meetings was held by the various Senate committees, according to official sources. (This was six working days. *Diario de los Debates*, April 18, 1995, p. 3; April 24, 1995, p. 25, April 25, 1995: 12, 14–16, and 20.) The Senate committees produced some 200 modifications to the executive's reform proposals before the bill was passed into law by unanimous vote of the Senate (105 in favor, 0 against) (*Diario de los Debates*, April 25, 1995: 26). The unanimous vote was partly the result of the leftist opposition political party—Party of the Democratic Revolution—(PRD)'s walk-out of the Senate and refusal to participate in official legislative politics of the bill (*Diario de los Debates*, April 25, 1995: 14).

4. Mexico has amended its constitution approximately 91 times since 1917. Carlos Arellano Garcia, *Juicio de Amparo*, Editorial Porrua, UNAM, 1978, chp. 2.

5. In its platform for electoral reform, the PRD has called for "eliminating the 'state of exception' in the ambit of electoral justice with the ultimate end of subjecting electoral acts to the constitutional control of the Supreme Court vis-a-vis the subjection of electoral laws to constitutional review and for the Court to possess the capacity to hear cases of alleged violations of individual electoral rights." Point 11, *Reforma Electoral Democratica*, 84 Points, Parliamentary Group of the PRD, Original Proposals of the PRD, March 27, 1996.

6. The most common violations of individual human rights by state authorities are violations of what Marshall (1963) called "civil rights" and include violations of prisoners' rights, abuse of authority, illegal detention by the judicial police, delay by the agents of the general prosecutor to make the accused appear before the court, refusal to render health services at public institutions, false accusations and indictment, medical malpractice, denial of the constitutional right to petition, and torture (Oropeza, 1995: 18).

7. Ernesto Zedillo, *Las politicas del bienestar*, Mexico, Partido Revolucionario Institucional, 1994:101–21. Zedillo first announced the 1994 Judicial Reforms in a speech on July 14, 1994. The PAN went on to win the first opposition gubernatorial victory in the state of Jalisco in the February 1995 elections, *Latin American Research Reports*, RM-95-03, March 1995: 5.

8. Hector Fix-Fierro, "La Reforma Judicial de 1994 y Las Acciones de Inconstitucionalidad," pp. 55–56, in *Transicion Politica y reforma constitucional en Mexico*, edited by Jaime F. Cardenas Gracia (Mexico City: UNAM, 1994). On this point, Zedillo is trying to "modernize" the Mexican judiciary to bring it in line with the dominant judicial models of the advanced industrial West. In Germany, for example, similarly reforms allowing the political minority to bring up cases for constitutional review turned the Federal constitutional tribunal into a state institutionalized oppositional instrument. Luca Mezzetti, *Giustizia costituzionale ed opposizione parlamentare. Modelli europei a confronto;* Rimini, Maggioli Editore, 1992:92, 246.

9. *The Washington Post*, March 12, 1995, A19. The article quotes a senior official in the Clinton White House.

10. This is also evidence of manner in which the 1994 reforms restrict the Court's ability to hear cases for judicial review brought forward only by members of the legislature, a procedure that excludes direct petition from citizens or citizens' groups. Although a citizen can still petition the Court to declare a law unconstitutional, as has happened four times during the 1994–96 period, the Court's decision continues to have no precedential value. It is also evident in the actual number of times the Court declared a law unconstitutional in the post-1994 judicial reform period. The Court found only two laws unconstitutional in two years—the retroactive tax law and the law of forced corporate affiliation, neither of which has precedential value. *La Jornada* May 22, 1995; August 11, 1995 (Tax Law); *Proceso,* 980, August 14, 1995: 32–36 (Corporate Affiliation).

11. *Proceso,* 1016, April 22, 1996: 16–22; *Semanario Judicial de la Federacion y Su Gaceta*, Novena Epoca, Tomo III, June 1996: 459–517. In this latter ruling, however, the Court's decision lacked any punitive sanction to its ruling because article 97 has no provision for guaranteeing coercive control over lack of compliance with its resolutions, *La Jornada,* June 1, 1996.

Chapter 4

The Struggle for Political Citizenship
Rights in Mexico's Delayed Transition
to Democracy (1988–99)

Why, when a regime is undergoing change, do social actors of different orientations and values reach agreement on the need to juridify political rights and to extend the right to a secret vote? Current theorists of democratization tend to analyze social actors' motives in terms of dichotomized alternatives involving conflict versus consensus. Conflict theorists, to explain the behavior of actors in regime transitions, invoke the idea of social actors guided by Machiavellian *fortuna* or uncertainty, contingency, and the unpredictability of social actors who wish to maximize their interests (Przeworski 1986; Schmitter and Karl 1994:174). According to this view, democracy is the product of a truce between conflicting groups that have achieved relative but temporary parity (Rex 1961).

In sharp contrast, consensus theorists propose Durkheimian integrative norms, moral sense, empathy, and mutual trust as the central social facts explaining the sources of democracy (Edles 1995). Democracy occurs because actors make the transition from the particularistic attachments of kinship and blood to a system of universalistic rules. Particular officeholders and policies may change in this system, but the citizens' ultimate loyalty is to the "overarching rules" of the constitutional legal order (Alexander 1991:167–69).

In this chapter I attempt a synthetic approach to the analysis of democratizing social action by examining the multivocal democratizing strategies and intentions of social actors involved in extending political citizenship rights in Mexico's democratization (1988–99). I argue that the process-oriented democratizing strategies of diverse social actors—insurgent indigenous groups, civic movement actors, regime political elites, opposition leaders—exemplify a motivational paradox of social action. According to this paradox, social actors agree on process-oriented democratizing strategies such as greater calculability in the exercise of political rights, juridic protection for autonomous rights of internal self-determination, the secret ballot, and the overall extension of the vote to previously unenfranchised groups of citizens. Yet they diverge radically on the substantive dimensions of these citizenship rights, such as the demand for greater social justice. Social actors with multifaceted, often conflicting motives agree on process-oriented strategies to ensure the extension of formal political rights, but they do not necessarily agree on substantive content, where motives are always mixed and can involve contradictory ethical, political, utilitarian, and instrumental aspects.

I conclude that in the Mexican case, the effort to extend political citizenship rights, an important dimension of democratization (Collins 1998), has advanced with regard to the free exercise of existing political rights, including the right to a secret vote. Nevertheless, the extension of new political rights, such as the vote abroad and the further juridification of political rights to self-government by indigenous actors, is impeded when conflicts arise between social actors dedicated to a content-oriented strategy of maximizing social justice with these rights and social actors who adhere to a process-oriented strategy serving the continuity and predictability of modern law and administration. Examples include struggles over the demand of indigenous insurgents in Chiapas for municipal self-government, and conflict surrounding the timing of the extension of the vote abroad and the appropriate size of the new national electorate living abroad.

THE COMPARATIVE-HISTORICAL SOCIOLOGICAL STUDY OF POLITICAL CITIZENSHIP

In this chapter I add to work by scholars of the comparative history of the state who have examined the extension of political citizenship rights in democratizing nations by showing how this extension applies to recent transitions to democracy (Mann 1987; Marshall 1963; Rokkan 1961; Therborn 1979, 1990).

Marshall's (1963) seminal account of the sequence in which citizenship rights were granted—civil, political and social—remains a landmark sociological study of the extension of political rights (Halsey 1984; Lipset 1973; Lockwood 1974; Turner 1986). Marshall posited that civil citizenship emerged in the eighteenth century; it was composed of "rights necessary for individual freedom—liberty of the person, freedom of speech, thought and faith, the right to own property and to conclude valid contracts, and the right to justice" (1963:71). Political citizenship emerged in the nineteenth century: "the right to participate in the exercise of political power, as a member of a body invested with political authority or as an elector of the members of such a body" (Marshall 1963:72). According to Marshall (1963:89–90), the extension of political citizenship rights involves an entire "pack-age" of related rights including the free exercise of the right to vote by the newly enfranchised and/or lower classes, social education aimed at breaking down the elitist idea that members of government should be drawn only from the upper classes, and the removal of the effects, in elections, of the unequal distribution of wealth through a reduction in bribery and corruption, and through the limitation of election expenses. The third stage, social citizenship, developed over the twentieth century as "the whole range from the right to a modicum of economic welfare and security to the right to share to the full in the social heritage and to live the life of a civilized being according to the standards prevailing in the society" (1963:72). Social citizenship is now known by the terms *social democracy* and *the welfare state* (Mann 1987:339).

In the history of Europe, Rokkan (1961, 1970) also conducted a comparative historical sociological analysis of the extension of political citizenship rights, particularly suffrage rights. In the British case, Rokkan (1961:142–43) argued that the institutional privacy protections of the secret ballot were demanded by the working-class Chartist movement as a way of reducing intimidation and the bribery of voters by their superiors, and/or as a way of reducing peers' pressures for conformity and solidarity. In most northwestern European countries, the effort was made in the late nineteenth and early twentieth centuries to develop standardized administrative procedures in the electoral process: the establishment of registers, the determination of voting rights, the maintenance of order at the polling stations, the casting of the vote, the recording of the act in the register, the counting of choices, the calculation of outcomes. Rokkan (1970:152–53) associates the standardization of the electoral process with literate, urban society because it introduces anonymity, specificity, and abstraction into the system of political interchange.

Despite these important insights into the development of Western European political citizenship rights, an account of citizenship that relies on ordering the extension of rights—civil rights first, political rights second, and finally social rights—relies too heavily on the Anglo experience. Mann (1987) argues that the British strategy of citizenship described by Marshall is only one of five pursued by advanced industrial European countries over the nineteenth and twentieth centuries; these include liberalism (Britain, the United States); reformism (France, Spain, Italy, Scandinavia); authoritarian monarchy (Germany, Austria, Russia, Japan); and fascist and authoritarian socialism (Nazi Germany and the Soviet Union). Similarly, the sociology of law has focused largely on the extension of property and civil rights in the Anglo-historical context (Aubert 1983; Dicey 1982; Fine 1984; Marsh 1961; Raz 1979). Scholars have not yet extensively explored the role of institutions such as the Supreme Court in legally guaranteeing the extension of political citizenship rights, especially in late-twentieth-century Hispanic societies (Abel 1988; Abel and Lewis 1995; Fine 1984).

DELAYED TRANSITIONS TO POLITICAL CITIZENSHIP AT THE END OF THE TWENTIETH CENTURY

At the end of the twentieth century, political citizenship rights are being extended in single-party regimes such as those in Tunisia, Mexico, Taiwan, Malaysia, Botswana, and Eastern Europe. These "third wave" transitions to democracy (Huntington 1991) are occurring in authoritarian single-party systems where social and civil rights, and even rights to participate, were conceded relatively early in the life of the regime. In Taiwan's democratization, for example, greater political opposition has been allowed to develop in the context of a slow increase in opposition parties' competition with the dominant party, which began in the late 1970s (Cheng 1989:474). In Malaysia, opposition parties have had the legal right to compete with the dominant party since the 1950s. Only recently, however, have they been strong enough to control money donations to the dominant political party as a strategy to further democratize the political system (Gomez 1996:81). In Tunisia, where social and civil citizenship rights were conceded early in the life of the authoritarian regime, the full constellation of political citizenship rights has been the last to emerge with increasing democratization (Anderson 1991:247).

The current cases therefore represent *delayed* transitions from authoritarian rule to fuller political citizenship rights, at least in comparison with the European cases of democratization on which much of the literature is based (Mann 1987; Marshall 1963; Rokkan 1961). Thus, in the sociological study of political citizenship in the third wave of democratization, we must focus on the interaction of the current establishment of new political rights with the social struggle for the *free exercise of existing political rights*. In many of these single-party regimes, the expansion of electoral competition has been an important component of current democratization. As a result, issues concerning the free exercise of existing political rights have been brought to the fore, such as the effort to reduce the role of money politics in election campaigns, minorities' right to unimpeded political self-determination, and the free exercise of suffrage rights (Kymlicka 1998:174–79).

At the same time, however, social struggles over new political citizenship rights are part of an ongoing process that includes the potentially pathbreaking extension of suffrage abroad, in the late 1990s, to millions of disenfranchised Mexican citizens (*Factor Tiempo* 1999). Similarly, the creation of new political rights is entailed in the extension of dual citizenship rights and in the effort by Mexican indigenous insurgents to ensure juridic protection for new claims to political participation through sovereign self-government (Stavenhagen 1995:12).

In analyzing the delayed extension of full political citizenship in the late twentieth century, one must account for the fusion of party and state, a central characteristic of modern authoritarian states (Janos 1970; Moore 1970). Such analysis requires attention to the relationship between the party-state, the political opposition, and civic groups regarding institutionalized practices of fraud—vote buying, bribery, and electoral violence—which compromise and delay the full exercise of existing suffrage rights. Furthermore, one must examine and understand the rise of conflicts and tensions that impede the extension of new political rights, such as indigenous rights to self-government and the extension of the suffrage abroad.

THE MEXICAN CASE

Mexico is a modern authoritarian state characterized by a complex array of legal, political, and administrative relationships that include the linkage of the dominant single party to the state. One example of such a linkage is the institutional relationship between suffrage rights and the legal system. Historically, electoral justice in Mexico has been administrative justice, ultimately subject only to party-state control. This situation is the result of the Supreme Court's weak role in relation to the Mexican executive, and of its century-old self-exclusion from the constitutional review of elections and the legitimation of the electoral process (Barragán 1994; Oropeza 1995). In electoral matters, the constitution has not stood as the highest authority over the Mexican political system. That authority has rested with the president, as leader of the nation and of the nation's dominant political party (Garrido 1989:420).

In legal terms, this highly anomalous situation has created the serious legal problem known since Roman times as *Judex non potest esse testis in propria causa* (The judge cannot be a witness in his own case), in which the authority is judge and party at the same time (Oropeza 1995:14). Because historically the Supreme Court and the federal judiciary are excluded from the process of electoral justice, the democratizing opposition political parties (PAN, PRD) have been forced to directly contest the validity of any given election with the interior minister or his associates. As a result, the ultimate judge of any election outcome has also been a member of the dominant political party (the PRI), who has an interest in not overturning the PRI's electoral victory (Fix-Zamudio and Cossio Diaz 1995:274–75). The opposition, realizing its weak legal position, has tried to strengthen its case by staging protests of electoral outcomes, including attempts to block PRI government officials' access to municipal and state government offices. Frequently the blockages have resulted in violent confrontations between the opposition and the PRI members, entailing property damage and death (PRD 1996).[1]

Below I show how the intrinsic institutional party-state connection further shapes multiple aspects of the broader social struggle for political citizenship rights: (1) through civic groups' efforts to sever the party-state connection in the administrative justice of electoral law (Aguayo 1995); (2) through the efforts of reformist authoritarian elites to extend the secret ballot within the dominant party (PRI) itself (Gordillo 1998); (3) through the effort of intellectuals and opposition-party members to extend the secret ballot to Mexican citizens abroad (Ross Pineda 1999); and (4) through indigenous groups' efforts to redefine a juridic framework with the Mexican state, based on radical democratic claims (EZLN *Reformas* 1996). I attempt to analyze the social effort both to extend new political rights and to ensure the effective exercise of existing political rights in Mexico. As suggested earlier, such a dualistic struggle for political citizenship is also occurring in other bureaucratized late-twentieth-century authoritarian states undergoing democratization, such as Taiwan, Malaysia, Tunisia, Zambia, Tanzania, Zimbabwe, Kenya, Cuba, and Singapore.

THEORETICAL APPROACH TO THE EXTENSION OF POLITICAL CITIZENSHIP RIGHTS: THE TENSION BETWEEN PROCESS-ORIENTED AND CONTENT-ORIENTED STRATEGIES OF SOCIAL ACTION

I argue that the social struggle for the extension of political citizenship rights is subject to the dialectic tension between content-oriented and process-oriented approaches to justice. Because the modern state is based on the abstract and universalist principles of legality, the dialectic of formal and substantive rationalization in the context of modern law and administration unfolds in a formal situation in which the law is applied in two different modes (Schluchter 1979:108–15).

Content-oriented or substantively rational action involves a mixed set of motives including mutually contradictory ethical, political, utilitarian, and instrumental aspects (Alexander 1983:156–57; Levine 1985:5–26; Schluchter 1979:11–643; Weber 1978:657). Although this situation implies tensions and contradictions between distinctive means and substantively rational ends, the maximization of social justice is often the primary goal of content-oriented strategies. In sociological terms, intellectuals and the nonprivileged often favor a strategy of the ethical maximization of social justice (Schluchter 1981:114).

Process-oriented action, on the other hand, implied by processes of formal rationalization, involves (in theory) an increase in formal logic, clarity, and generality of legal rules, and thereby an increase in calculability (Factor and Turner 1994:139–42; Weber 1978:656–57). Behavior oriented toward formally rational goals involves a "simpler" agenda in that action need be aimed only toward greater calculability and/or theoretical systematization (Kalberg 1980:1152–55; Swidler 1973:38). In sociological terms, professionals and those in charge of rational economic and political enterprises often adopt strategies whose results support the continuity and predictability of modern law and administration.[2]

I claim here that social actors can agree on process-oriented, formal rationalizing ends without necessarily agreeing on content-oriented, substantively rational goals. For example, wherever social actors converge to promote the secret ballot, they must agree at the level of formal procedural rationality. Nevertheless, they do not necessarily agree in regard to substantive content, where motives are always mixed.

Indeed, a central tension in Weberian thought is the point that formal rationality and its predictability or calculability both compromise and are compromised by the substantive demands of social justice that emerge from social actors' content-oriented strategies. In the Mexican case that follows, I make two related arguments with respect to the extension of political citizenship.

First, I argue that although formal rationalization in legal decision-making has increased, there has been no decrease in substantively rational goals of the cultural actors pressing for the free ballot. This paradox is illustrated in the actions of urban, literate, civil society actors in classic "civil" movements, who converge in relatively heterogeneous social coalitions in support of the secret ballot because they agree in regard to formal procedurality but have different substantive agendas based on distinctive content-oriented goals. The formal convergence of various social actors with differing substantive goals is the result of their support for the notion of calculability in exercising the franchise. The secret ballot is a formal ballot: It is administered in accordance with clear, predictable, abstract (depersonalized) results and expresses a formal rationalizing tendency. Nevertheless, social actors desire an increase in the calculability of the administrative procedures associated with the secret ballot because it enhances the likelihood of support for their respective substantive goals, which include the greater valuation of individual, human, political, and social rights.

Even the secret ballot itself can be viewed as one such substantive goal when it is perceived as a political right in itself. This is the case especially when the franchise is treated in ethical terms, as a form of freedom of choice or of nonviolent resolution of conflict.

Second, I argue that further examples of such actors' content-oriented strategies to extend political rights include multiple social actors' convergence on the extension of the franchise to Mexicans living in the United States and indigenous groups' desire to juridify political rights to autonomous self-government. The indigenous insurgents' social struggle for juridic security is intended to ensure the legal right to political autonomy and self-government within the territory of the Mexican nation (Díaz Polanco 1991; EZLN *Reformas* 1996). The social effort to extend the franchise to Mexicans living abroad is the result of a complex set of mixed motives: the opposition groups' anticipated desire to win elections; the state officials' desire to extend dual citizenship protection to disenfranchised Mexicans living abroad; and a commitment by Mexican and U.S. intellectuals, civil actors, and others to the principle of the extension of the suffrage to previously unenfranchised groups.

In the Mexican case, I demonstrate the general dialectical tension between process-oriented and content-oriented objectives in four social dimensions of political citizenship: (1) in the emergence of the political rights movement with multiple substantive objectives, including the attempt to sever party-state control over electoral monitoring and to bring Mexico's institutions into line with worldwide democratizing trends; (2) in regime incumbents' effort to allow secret voting in open PRI primaries so that party members can vote for reformist candidates without fear of punishment by their hard-line peers, and vice versa; (3) in the effort of Mexican and U.S. intellectuals, regime elites, and opposition politicians to ensure the extension of the franchise abroad, with the cultural goal of extending the suffrage to previously unenfranchised citizens and the political goal of winning electoral votes; and (4) in indigenous groups' effort to juridify formal political rights in order to ensure rights to self-government.

THE ROLE OF CIVIC ACTORS IN PROMOTING THE SECRET BALLOT

In Mexico's electoral situation, nongovernmental "political rights" movements involving the extension of legal and political rights have emerged in the recent wave of democratization in Mexico (1988–99). Civic Alliance, one of the most prominent of these democratizing movements, is a broad, heterogeneous coalition of antistate intellectuals, artists, teachers, reformist civil servants, journalists, clergy, and human rights advocates with mixed, substantively rational motives. These actors have converged to demand greater legality in the administration of the franchise as well as greater accountability of the government toward its citizens (Botz 1995:197; Pia Lara 1997:13–14).

The complex mixture of ethical and political motives in these alliances is evident in the multiplicity of motives for promoting political rights. One motive or set of motives includes the cultural aspirations of Mexican civil society actors in promoting a transition of the franchise from a status to a formal contract. This is manifested in the idea that the most important of all political rights is "the right to universal suffrage, equal, personal, free, secret and respected" (Malo 1994:20). Accordingly the problem is that "the separation of the fundamental interests of the majority from the interests of a powerful minority, the selection of candidates by local notables, restricted popular participation in base organizations, and, most notably, fraud" have caused a "progressive deterioration" of the act of suffrage in Mexico evident in lack of voter interest, voter apathy, and abstentionism (Malo 1994:25). Because fraud violates the political right to the secret ballot, democratizing organizations such as the Civic Alliance began in the early 1990s to call for electoral observation as necessary for the defense of free suffrage (Alianza Cívica 1994).

Another substantively rational motive for participating in electoral observation is based on an ethical claim by members of human rights organizations within the coalition, namely that "political rights" are a subset of individual "human rights" and are subject to protection as such. According to this claim, international human rights law grants human rights groups the right and the responsibility to ensure that state officials administer the vote impartially, and that practices such as vote buying or exchanging political patronage for an individual's vote cease.[3]

Another form of substantive social justice based on ethical considerations is the effort to teach "political rights" or to "conscientize" members of the nonprivileged classes as to their suffrage rights. The urban, highly literate character of Civic Alliance's membership is reflected in the high levels of education in the movement (5 percent doctorates, 16 percent master's degrees, 79 percent bachelor's degrees, 95 percent at least some university education) and in the large proportion of academics and teachers (32 percent) (Lear McConnell 1996).[4] Through civic education, members hope to use the franchise as a way of teaching voters to treat the vote as a formally rational contract freed of fraternal elements, and thus to overturn class prejudice (Alianza Cívica 1994).

The use of the franchise to teach political rights is a form of substantive justice based on ethical considerations, as reflected clearly in this statement by Civic Alliance movement leader Sergio Aguayo:

All [of our activities] are an exercise in civic education. I mean, it is important to be able to prove that there was, or there is, an irregularity. But it is even more important to get the people to vote, as many as possible because that becomes an education in the concept of citizenship and human dignity. . . . [These are] ideas which underlie what we have been doing. I have a very clear idea of what we are doing. . . . I am not naive. I have lived long enough to realize that we are moving in a dimension that is indestructible. . . . It is very, very solid. We are not competing for power. That is the main reason for our success, in my opinion.

[You mean that you are not a political party?] No! We are moving at the level of principles and that is new in Mexican politics, at least as far as these kinds of movements are concerned, because most of them started as nonpartisan and sometime thereafter they show that they are really interested in power politics.

[You mentioned that you have always believed that intellectuals had a "social responsi- bility." Where does this principle of the social responsibility of the intellectual come from?] I suppose that there is some genetic impact somewhere in my family. Part of my family were rebels, religious rebels in Jalisco, but . . . no . . . ever since I was a child, I didn't like injustices. I have had to fight injustices for a number of personal and family reasons. So, I developed a sensibility to those things, and ever since I have learned how to fight and to be more and more successful. . . . I am in basic agreement with the dignity of human beings and individual human beings and the Universal Declaration of Human Rights. It is a beautiful chapter—a set of principles. I have always [been] very clear that my public life, and my private life if you like, is to move myself, my society, and my country in that direction. It is very simple. It has nothing to do with ideas or intellectuality. It has to do with ethics. (Personal interview, August 27, 1996)

Civic education is substantively rational because the promotion of political rights entails promoting the rights of the marginalized on the basis of ethical norms derived from an internal moral framework (Malo 1994:16). This idea is consistent with the assumption that the creation of rights as a "source of power which even a hitherto entirely powerless person may possess" is linked historically to an internal, voluntary element developed "almost everywhere under religious influences" (We- ber 1978:213; also see Alexander 1983:114).[5]

THE INSTITUTIONAL CONSEQUENCES OF THE EFFORTS OF CIVIC MOVEMENTS FOR DEMOCRATIC ACCOUNTABILITY

The desire of the Civic Alliance and of human rights and other democratizing organizations to continue their electoral monitoring reflects the larger, complex, difficult problem of how to overturn *Judex non potest esse testis in propria causa* in already modern bureaucratized states.[6] Because this cultural effort to sever the party-state connection is based on a complex mix of substantive motives, one should not predict a linear evolution to a greater formal, rational, legal systematization of law. It is more likely that conflicts will arise between the rules promoted by democratizing social actors and the laws already in place in the authoritarian regime. As a result, the legal institutionalization of changes to electoral justice will involve a complex back-and-forth process of legal reasoning, fluctuating between substantively rational, substantively irrational, formally irrational, and formal rational approaches to law. In the Mexican case, this fluctuation is also evident in matters of legal decision-making.

To protect the suffrage, Mexican intellectuals, artists, civil servants, and members of human rights movements developed domestic forms of electoral monitoring techniques learned abroad. They monitored elections during the 1991–97 period to ensure administrative impartiality in all aspects of the campaign process: political advertising, media exposure, election-day procedures, and quick counting of the vote, which has formal rationalizing institutional consequences (Aguayo 1995:160). In its review of elections, the Civic Alliance publishes its reports of documented cases of vote buying, and makes statements about the relative "cleanness" of an election. In the 1994 presidential elections, these statements were taken seriously by the United States and foreign governments as objective reviews of the actual level of fraud, and hence as indicators of the degree of legitimacy to accord to the election itself ("Civic Alliance Queries" 1994; Fox and Hernandez 1995:30–31). In formally reviewing the legality and legitimacy of elections, these organizations serve as proxy for an impartial supreme court.[7]

The *Judex non potest . . .* problem resurfaced when the Mexican government sought to control international funding to democratizing nongovernment organizations for electoral monitoring. The electoral administration told the Civic Alliance that it must cease its substantively ethically based monitoring of elections because continued observation implied the role of judge in electoral processes and would make the Civic Alliance both "party" and "judge" ("Civic Alliance Cannot Have Electoral Monitors" 1997; "IFE: Only" 1997). The Civic Alliance was unwilling to follow these administrative guidelines on the grounds that it was not seeking political power through the support of political candidates and because of its apparent perception that the electoral administration's legal reforms were not actually legal/formal. This reaction illustrates how no decrease has occurred in the substantively rational goals of the cultural actors pressing for the free ballot, despite an increase in formal argumentation in legal decision-making by the electoral administration.

The cultural effort to promote the franchise as a formal contract has continued in Mexico. Initially, Supreme Court justices failed to provide juridic security for electoral rights by codifying the franchise as a full formal contract. On November 1, 1995 a simple majority of Supreme Court justices (six of 11) agreed that electoral material should be subject to constitutional review. Also, the Court should establish a definite criterion for "electoral material" because the 1917 constitution did not establish a "defense mechanism" for citizens' political rights in the face of the supposed unconstitutionality of such a law ("Although" 1996:35; "Results" 1995). Nevertheless, the minority opinion was that the Court still should refrain from reviewing and checking the legitimacy of elections ("Results" 1995:1).

One Supreme Court minister justified the Court's continued self-restraint and refusal to act as a constitutional arbiter as the result of an old fear that resurfaced in the October-November 1995 debates on the Court's role of reviewing electoral laws. Minister Castro y Castro argued as follows:

A Court which has no army, that doesn't control the budget, and that doesn't manage foreign relations, could only with great difficulty put itself over the other two powers. Everything is in the hands of the Executive, and the moment that the Court might want to put itself above the other two powers, very simply and easily the president, who is the natural head of the Army, would simply do away with the Court. ("Although" 1996:36)

Although electoral justice still operates principally according to formal administrative code (Becerra 1997), a 1996 political pact brought in a new generation of leaders of the Federal Electoral Council (IFE). This pact gave the counselors voting power and reduced the political parties to nonvoting status in the council. This was a strong democratizing step, given the historical lack of full multiparty competition in Mexico and the public perception of electoral justice by administrative code was historically perceived of as "conservative," "partial," or "officialist" justice (pro-PRI).[8]

The historical July 1997 elections marked a turning point in the administration of elections because they were the first federal elections organized by an autonomous authority, the Federal Electoral Institute (IFE); it is generally accepted that the results were honest (Aguayo 1998a:172). Thus the post-1997 period is viewed as a watershed in the democratization of Mexico, even though the *Judex non potest* . . . problem persists in the administration of electoral justice in some states.

This transition was importantly propelled forward by the urban, highly literate social actors' cultural aspirations in promoting nonviolent forms of political fraternization; by a transition in the franchise toward greater calculability of the vote; and by the conformity of Mexico's institutions to general worldwide trends. Paradoxically, however, this process-oriented democratizing strategy is also a consequence of the substantive goals of democratic elites, because an increase in the calculability of the administrative procedures associated with the secret ballot increases the likelihood of support for these elites' substantive goals. Yet despite an increase in formal rationalization in legal decision-making due to the shift in the franchise from status to formal contract, we find no decrease in the substantively rational goals of the cultural actors pressing for expanded political rights.

These tensions are evident in the activities of Civic Alliance after 1997. The overall strengthening of civil society through increased, more objective media attention to elections, better-informed voters, exit polls, and preelection polls led to more selective electoral observation efforts by Civic Alliance members. As election authorities became more autonomous and as the political opposition governed more states and municipalities, electoral decision-making became more formally rational. At the same time, however, one sees the continuing absorption of nongovernment organization (NGO) actors, with their ongoing substantive concerns, into the government itself. By 1997, for example, the voter registration lists, which had been marked by a long history of manipulation and abuse, were no longer a source of concern: The 1997 leader of the electoral registry was one of the founders of Civic Alliance (Aguayo 1998a:172). In early 1988, three of seven founders of Civic Alliance held public office: one as a PRD federal deputy and two as members of the Federal District government headed by PRD leader Cuauhtemoc Cardenas (Aguayo 1998a:185). Thus one sees that an increase in the calculability of the administrative procedures associated with the secret ballot (such as more autonomous electoral institutions and cleaner elections) leads to greater support for such actors' substantive goals (as in their election and appointment to public office).

Furthermore, although formal rationalization in legal decision-making increased because of the shift in the franchise from status to formal contract, we find no decrease in the substantively rational goals of the cultural actors pressing for expanded political rights. This is evident in the shift in Civic Alliance's substantive priorities in the period after 1997. As the 2000 presidential election approaches, elections appear to be increasingly less fraudulent, and to be administered in accordance with formally rational goals. The issue for Civic Alliance and other, similar NGOs is the extent to which they can maintain attention to formal electoral observation rather than to other substantive goals including the promotion of other forms of popular participation, referenda, the monitoring of public officials' conduct in office, and the promotion of a negotiated solution to the conflict in Chiapas (Aguayo 1998a:183). Therefore one sees continued dialectical tension between process-oriented and content-oriented objectives in the cultural effort to completely remove party-state control over electoral monitoring and to bring Mexico's institutions into line with worldwide democratizing trends.

THE SECRET BALLOT AND THE ROLE OF REFORMIST AUTHORITARIAN INCUMBENTS

Nevertheless, the effort to ensure calculability is not the only motive of social actors in promoting the secret ballot. Another key reason why actors agree on the secret ballot is the desire to protect themselves from potentially coercive pressure. Citizens, for instance, may prefer secrecy in order to protect themselves from peers who expect them to vote in a certain way. Indeed, Rokkan (1961:142–43) viewed the secret ballot, in its development in the West, as part of the process of reducing the influence of pressure on the individual voter, either by superiors or by peers.

In Mexico, President Zedillo and PRI party leaders recently have experimented with internal party reforms in an effort to avoid further fissures within the dominant party-state; to stem further losses of splinter groups to the opposition parties, such as occurred in the state elections in Zacatecas, Tlaxcala, and Baja California Sur (1997–98); and to restore the party's legitimacy (Gordillo 1998; Las elecciones primarias 1998; Dresser 1999). In one key reform, the PRI was allowed to hold open primaries for gubernatorial candidates in the states of Chihuahua, Tlaxcala, Tamaulipas, Puebla, and Sinaloa in which all voters, not only PRI members, were eligible to vote (Gordillo 1998:1). In Chihuahua, this innovation produced a highly regarded gubernatorial soft-liner candidate, Patricio Martinez, who defeated the PRI hard-liner candidate in the primaries (Lopez 1998). Martinez went on to defeat the six-year standing incumbent governor of the right-wing opposition party, PAN, in a relatively tight race. In the state of Tamaulipas, the direct vote of party militants produced another popular gubernatorial candidate, Tomas Yarrington Ruvalcaba, who was also the PRI governor's candidate (Las elecciones primarias 1998).

President Zedillo pledged to extend the idea of open candidate selection by secret vote to the 2000 presidential candidate (Dillon 1999) through a series of state primaries that would culminate in an American-style party convention. Thus he has proposed to break with the 60-year-old tradition of the *dedazo*, the president's hand-picked choice of his successor. Under the new system proposed by Zedillo, successive local primaries would result in the election of delegates, who later would meet representatives of the PRI labor, peasant, and other wings of the party to select the presidential candidate. In a historic decision made on May 17, 1999, the PRI membership voted to approve President Zedillo's plan for the first nationwide presidential primary, scheduled for November 7, 1999 (Dillon 1999). In theory, all eligible voters will be able to cast a secret ballot in all 300 of Mexico's electoral districts to select the PRI presidential candidate.

An argument based on "protection against peer pressure" seems to explain this behavior by Mexican ruling elites. The decision of PRI elites to hold open primaries and to take steps toward suffrage extension suggests that some ruling elites, at times of regime change, apparently wish to ensure the right to vote in favor of hard-line incumbent candidates and policies associated with the old regime without fear of punishment by others in society (Dillon 1999:6). Conversely, soft-line authoritarians (those in power who nonetheless push for political liberalization) want the right to vote for reformist candidates without the fear of punishment by their hard-line peers. In both cases, secrecy grants that right.

Indeed, even President Zedillo stressed the centrality of the secret vote when he first proposed the open primary system of candidate selection. On the eve of the PRI's seventieth anniversary, Zedillo declared: "I reiterate today with absolute clarity that I will not designate the PRI candidate. Our selection process should use the *popular secret vote* of our active members and all of our citizens who lean toward our party" (Dillon 1999:1; emphasis added).

The view of the secret ballot as a form of "protection" from superiors and peers also raises an interesting sociological paradox. It strongly suggests that to ensure the accountability of elected officers, authoritarian elites must rely on an institution, namely the secret ballot, that diminishes the accountability of the party member voters. In the privacy of the voting booth, party members are free to vote for candidates for whom they might not vote if voting occurred in an open forum, where social pressures for unanimity often prevail. In the 70-year history of the selection of PRI presidential candidates, party members have been subject to elite and sectoral pressure to agree unanimously with the outgoing president's choice in an open selection process (Garrido 1982:353–56; Meyer 1989:343).

By adopting the secret ballot as a formal institution, authoritarian elites in the late 1990s agree that it is a formal, private arena for political expression by actors with distinctive content-oriented, substantive agendas. These elites' agreement to extend the secret ballot within the party-state represents the convergence of social actors possessing different substantive motives (greater and lesser commitment to political liberalization) on a formal institution that ensures the private expression of their positions. Therefore the development of privacy procedures involving the secret ballot in periods of regime change is one institutional procedure for coping with uncertainty. If coping with uncertainty is perceived as only one of numerous motives for behavior in regime change, then the development of privacy protections associated with the secret ballot is consistent with conceptions of democratization as a process of institutionalizing bounded uncertainty (Schmitter and Karl 1994:176).

This convergence on the secret ballot by reformist authoritarian incumbents raises interesting questions for an understanding of democratic accountability because, in fact, the secret ballot diminishes the voters' accountability. This is precisely why no secret ballot exists in some of the Mexican indigenous communities in the states of Oaxaca and Chiapas (Aguirre Beltrán 1991:40–41). According to *usos y custumbres* (custom and law), political decisions still are made through open voting, in which we see the opposite type of convergence: social actors' agreement on the substantive, content-oriented goal of preserving the influence of peers and superiors in the act of voting (Santibáñez and Gonzalo 1997:19). As I discuss later, the dialectical tension between claims for formal, universalistic laws and laws based on ethnic particularism characterizes the indigenous insurgents' struggle for the expansion of political citizenship.

INTRAPARTY DEMOCRATIZATION: THE EMERGENCE OF ELECTORAL LEGITIMATION?

Finally, another aspect of authoritarian elites' extension of political citizenship rights in the late 1990s should be analyzed in relation to the establishment of the secret ballot in open PRI primary elections. Mexican critics of the PRI argue that in 1998–99, the "open primaries" method signifies a more democratic alternative to the *dedazo* method. Open primaries, however, have not resulted in true debates between candidates, nor in the systematic presentation of positions on issues. Nor have they been held in equitable conditions, because there are no rules preventing guaranteed victory for candidates with greater resources and/or candidates preferred by the interim governor (Las elecciones primarias 1998). Even PRI supporters of open primaries note that these primaries are associated with the increasing importance of candidates' personalities and personal biographies. On the other hand, PRI supporters observe with satisfaction that they have created a growing role for party-state social sectors in the selection of candidates (Gordillo 1998).

Neither critics nor proponents are certain whether the PRI's early efforts at open primaries express authoritarian or democratic elements; this uncertainty reveals the open primaries' transitional character. In Mexico, the selection of party-state leaders appears to be making a slow transition from the authoritarian designation of a successor by the president (the *dedazo* method) toward a more democratic recognition of the leader by the group (through election). Previous attempts to expand popular participation within the PRI (in 1964 and 1987) did not lead to widespread intraparty democratization, often because public demonstrations of internal party conflict were perceived of as dangerous by the party leadership to the party's image of unaminity and internal consensus (Scott 1964:142) and as potentially leading to the risk of outright schism and the creation of an alternative political party (Meyer 1989:341–43). Therefore predictions regarding the continuation of an intraparty democratizing trend have been cautious.

Nevertheless, current changes in the suffrage, tending toward the secret vote in the Mexican party-state, might well represent movement toward an antiauthoritarian interpretation of the bases for legitimation of the PRI, associated with modern democratization (Weber 1978:266–67). President Zedillo's efforts to ensure electoral victories for his soft-liner candidates through the secret vote in open party primaries reflect the use of an expanded suffrage both as an instrument of power and as a potential popular, egalitarian source of power (also see Therborn 1990:14). In theory, the electoral principle as a method of leadership selection implies legitimation by the will of the ruled, rather than by authoritarian designation. In Mexico, President Zedillo still tries to maintain significant influence over the selection process by making known his own preference for candidates, and probably also by influencing other early candidates to resign from the primary race, thereby clearing the way for his choice (*La Jornada* 1999).

Thus the back-and-forth process of democratizing leadership selection is also subject to the dialectic of process (formal) and content (substantive) rationalization. On one hand, the November 1999 primary elections for the PRI presidential candidate imply convergence on the principle of formal freedom in the selection of leadership, in that legitimacy would be formally derived from and maintained by the will of the ruled (Mommsen 1983:289–99). Further democratization of leadership, however, would imply substantive rationalization by expanding the scope for the influence of public opinion beyond the authority of officialdom (Cohen 1970:72). On the other hand, incumbent regime elites are not likely to allow formal freedoms in the selection of leaders to result in the significant loss of their political power. Thus the movement toward intraparty democratization of the PRI possesses two qualities simultaneously. First, it is a formal way of mobilizing mass sentiment in support of the party against the intellectuals' criticisms about its "undemocratic" character. Second, it is a substantive method for causing local groups to identify with the party and of promoting the turnover in governmental posts, of persons with distinctively reformist-democratizing positions (Huntington 1970:38–39; also see Gordillo 1998). This latter goal thereby slowly changes the legitimation of authority in favor of soft-liner authoritarian elites.

SHIFTING THE BOUNDARIES OF THE PEOPLE: EXTENDING THE SUFFRAGE ABROAD AND THE ETHNIC DEMAND FOR JURIDIC RIGHTS TO POLITICAL AUTONOMY

In Mexico, the meaning of the social struggle to extend full political citizenship rights clearly depends on who "the people" are (Therborn 1990). Debates over indigenous Mexicans' rights to full equality and their access to both political and social citizenship rights—or the beneficial share of the country's economic development promised to all citizens in the 1917 Constitution—have challenged what it means to be part of the Mexican nation ("Debate over Mexican Migrants" 1999). This is the case because the armed guerrilla movement that emerged in January 1994—the Zapatista Army of National Liberation (EZLN)—is also demanding the political right to internal self-determination and autonomous political sovereignty (EZLN *Reformas* 1996). At the same time, opposition parties of the left and the right, Mexican and U.S. intellectuals, and PRI moderates claim that the estimated seven million Mexican immigrants living in the United States are politically equal to Mexican nationals and thus should be included in national political life through dual citizenship, the right to the secret vote, and the right to join Mexican political parties. Tagle (1998) even argues that the demands for extending political citizenship rights in these two cases are intertwined: The presence of the Zapatistas in Chiapas accelerated the electoral reforms leading to the effort to extend the vote abroad. Other Mexican states also are witnessing an acceleration of the search for the formal juridification of indigenous rights.

EXTENDING THE SUFFRAGE ABROAD: ETHICAL MINIMALIZATION AND ETHICAL MAXIMALIZATION AS DISTINCTIVE SOCIAL STRATEGIES

The social struggle to extend the suffrage abroad is another example of divergent actors' convergence on process-oriented goals despite differences in substantive motives. Nearly 10 million potential Mexican voters live in the United States, including 7.1 million Mexican-born immigrants and 2.7 adult children of Mexican-born parents. Three out of four Mexican immigrants live in 33 counties in California, Arizona, Colorado, Texas, Illinois, Georgia, and New York; the other one-fourth are dispersed through the country and altogether these U.S. residents potentially represent 15 percent of the entire Mexican electorate (Dillon 1998).

The social response to the issue of the vote for Mexican migrants abroad emerged in connection with the 1996 consensus pact, when President Zedillo, the PRI, and opposition parties converged on the New Nationality Law. This law extended dual citizenship to all eligible Mexicans living in the United States, beginning in March 1998 (*Factor Tiempo* 1999).[9] The law largely grants to Mexican migrants living abroad civil rights to property ownership in Mexico, the right to buy and sell land, the right to educational benefits such as college education for their children in

Mexico, and the right to cross the U.S.-Mexican border without a tourist card (Rifkin 1998:4). Mexico thus follows the trend toward dual citizenship with the United States, such as exists with Colombia, the Dominican Republic, Canada, Ireland, France, and Poland ("Immigrants in U.S." 1996).

The Mexican political parties' unanimity regarding the dual citizenship law reflects their convergence on two content-oriented strategies, namely ethical maximization of social justice and the civil right to own property in Mexico. PRI senators argued that "those who are forced to work and live outside of Mexico because of adverse economic conditions often face unjust treatment despite the fact that they are productive members of society" ("Senate Unanimously Passes" 1996:2). Members of commissions on migration and financial issues, who designed the constitutional changes, hoped that the dual citizenship law would satisfy the needs of the many citizens who live abroad with the hope of returning to Mexico with financial resources. According to PRI Senator Amador Rodriguez Lozano, "Millions of Mexicans live abroad in unjust conditions . . . despite the financial contribution they make, they are denied opportunities based on the fact that they are not citizens" ("Senate Unanimously Passes" 1996:2).[10] President Zedillo suggested another central motive for the dual citizenship law, which helps to explain the multiple social actors' unanimous agreement on ethical maximization of social justice: He argued that the changes to the Constitution were prompted by "the anti-(Mexican) immigration atmosphere prevalent in the U.S." ("Expatriate Mexicans' Electoral Role" 1998:2).

Yet the issue of dual citizenship only raised the issue of Mexican migrants' voting rights; it did not guarantee citizens abroad the right to participate in political parties or to vote abroad. As a result of the July 1996 pact, Congress eliminated only Articles 35 and 36 from the Mexican Constitution; these required that Mexicans vote only in their home districts. Because of the lack of precedent for extending the franchise to approximately one to seven million citizens abroad, there was no legal referent for the organization of an election abroad, nor a budget for conducting such an election ("IFE Urges" 1998). In July 1996, to study the question further, the Mexican Congress authorized a commission of 13 specialists to analyze the technical hurdles that have delayed voting abroad, and to report on their findings.

In anticipation of the special commission's November 1998 report, and in an effort to fill the juridic gap that emerged because the vote abroad still lacked a legal referent, Mexican and international intellectuals, opposition parties of the left and the right, and Mexican migrants living in the United States agreed on the vote abroad for a variety of rational substantive reasons. Many intellectuals thought the extension of the suffrage abroad would pave the way for the greater exercise of substantive citizenship rights, including social rights. Intellectuals supported the vote abroad for substantive cultural reasons. Emilio Zebadua, a Mexican intellectual in charge of the IFE support group for the special commission, argued that extending the vote abroad would bring Mexico's institutions "up with the modern world" and would be a "delayed recognition of the globalization that characterizes the modern world" (*La Jornada* 1998a:2). UNAM social science professor Leticia

Chelius viewed the extension of the vote abroad as recognition of Mexico's diversity, which would put Mexico "within the context of global framework" (*Excelsior* 1998b:2). Mexican intellectual Silvia Gomez Tagle, a citizen electoral advisor, argued that Mexico was "arriving late to democracy and needed mechanisms [including the vote abroad] that permit equity and transparency in all processes" (*Excelsior* 1998b:2). Arturo Santamaria, a political science professor at UNAM, believed that the vote abroad would reinforce Mexican democracy and would protect an otherwise unprotected Mexican population in the United States (*Excelsior* 1998b). U.S. political scientist Wayne Cornelius supported the vote abroad as part of the general democratic transition in Mexico (Dillon 1998:5). Michel Ayala, representative to the U.N. Program on Development, stated that the vote abroad was one of the most important international issues because it dealt with extending political rights to nationals beyond national boundaries (*La Jornada* 1998b).

Another substantive or content-oriented reason for supporting the vote abroad was expressed by opposition parties of the left, who argued that it was part of the general historical process of extending the suffrage. One PRD party spokesperson explained the party's position in favor of the vote abroad as "in favor of democracy, for the right of all to vote and be voters, just like the advances in the past such as giving the vote to youth and to women, and now to Mexicans living abroad" (Incorporar el Voto 1998:1). The opposition rightist party (PAN) also favors the vote abroad: Panista Ernesto Ruffo Appel, the first non-PRI governor in Mexico (1989–95, Baja California), said that he supported the vote abroad because he perceives that migrants may vote against the PRI, and thus for the opposition (Dillon 1998; Incorporar el Voto 1998).

Mexican citizens living abroad thought the extension of the suffrage abroad would pave the way for the greater exercise of substantive citizenship rights, including social rights. An estimated 83 percent of Mexicans living in the United States want to vote in Mexican elections (Dillon 1998). One Mexican migrant living in the United States, who traveled to Mexico City to lobby for the right to vote abroad, commented: "Before it didn't matter much whether we voted or not, but [now], the people themselves are reforming Mexico, and that has made it matter. I can't vote either in the U.S. or in Mexico. . . . And yet we Mexicans in the U.S. send $5 billion every year back home to our families. We want a say" (Smith 1998:A19). Another Mexican, a U.S. resident since 1974 who came from a rural area in Michoacán to seek "a better horizon for our families," viewed the formal vote abroad as a potential means of maximizing social justice. He stated, "We want our political voice so we can contribute and make Mexico stronger, and make the economy stronger so young people won't have to leave like we did" (Smith 1998:A19).

Thus agreement on the social effort to extend the franchise to Mexicans living abroad is also the result of a complex set of mixed motives: opposition groups' anticipated desire to win elections; state officials' desire to extend dual citizenship protection to disenfranchised Mexicans living abroad; the commitment to the principle of extending the suffrage to previously unenfranchised groups, held by Mexican and U.S. intellectuals, civil actors, and others; and the perception, held by Mexican migrants in the United States, that the formal vote abroad will pave the way for greater social justice.

In March 1999, leaders of the "Pro-Mexican Vote 2000" organization, which represents diverse social organizations of Mexican migrants in the United States, lobbied and interviewed Mexican party leaders of the Chamber of Deputies, members of the Senate, IFE administrators, and even the PRI Secretary of the Interior. They found initial consensus regarding the extension of the vote abroad (*Factor Tiempo* 1999).

Nevertheless, members of the party-state PRI do not unanimously support the vote abroad. Mariano Palacios Alcocer, president of the national committee of the PRI, disputed the 615-page final report of the congressional commission that the vote abroad for the 2000 presidential election was "strong, legitimate and logistically viable" and that the proposal "complies with the juridic rationality of Mexico's electoral system" (*La Jornada* 1998:1). Alcocer argued that the vote abroad for the 2000 election was not viable because the current proposal did not meet the requirement of transitory Article 8 of the law: That article required a National Registry of Citizens as a precondition to exploring the vote abroad (*Excelsior* 1998a). One PRI senator classified the special commission's report as "deceiving, incomplete, partisan, verging toward the Left opposition's [PRD's] position and lacking in intellectual honesty" (quoted in *Reforma* 1998:1). PRI hardliners argued that the right to the vote abroad should not be extended because it "represents a threat to Mexican national sovereignty" ("Expatriate Mexicans' Electoral Role" 1998). Some polls and political experts suggest that the vote abroad may largely be an anti-PRI vote, which might even offer the opportunity to unseat the PRI (Dillon 1998); this prediction, however, is by no means certain (Faesler 1999).

Other social actors skeptical about the vote abroad include PRI civil servants, constitutional scholars, and some U.S. intellectuals. The latter fear attacks on Mexican migrants by racist or nationalistic U.S. citizens and/or by the U.S. Immigration and Naturalization Service (INS) if large-scale Mexican campaigning and voting take place on U.S. soil (Carpizo 1978; Dillon 1998). U.S. groups ("Absentee Vote Proposal" 1999) and some Mexican intellectuals (Smith 1998:A19) also have raised the problem of dual allegiance and the weakening of either U.S. or Mexican citizenship implied by the right to vote in both the United States and Mexico.

Thus the extension of the suffrage abroad is a social process that is also subject to the dialectic tension between content-oriented and process-oriented approaches to justice. Critical intellectuals, Mexican intellectuals or citizen electoral counselors, some PRI moderates, Mexican migrants, and opposition political parties of the right and the left have converged on the content-oriented strategy of ethical maximization of social justice for the juridification and application of the law.

On the other hand, some PRI members, constitutional scholars, intellectuals who support the party-state government policies, U.S. nationalists, and U.S. intellectuals favor a strategy of "ethical minimization," which preserves the continuity and predictability of modern law and administration. As a result of this latter strategy, the extension of the vote abroad has been postponed until the 2006 presidential election because of its high cost (estimated between $76 and $356 million) and the lack of time (*Factor Tiempo* 1999).

The extension of the vote abroad is a new political right perceived as pathbreaking by some key members of the party-state, and viewed as potentially and actually threatening to the political interests of the PRI. The continued fusion of the party-state and the party-state's calculations that to win the presidential elections in 2000, it must oppose the extension of the vote abroad constitute a central motive for delay (Faesler 1999).

In addition, the perception that the extension of the vote abroad threatens the current nation's territorial integrity is a significant reason for delay in the extension of the suffrage. The right to vote in two countries may raise the central political problem of dual citizenship: the potential problem of divided allegiance (Brubaker 1998:133). Some members of the party-state object to the extension of the vote abroad because of the norm whereby state membership should be unique: that is, exhaustive and mutually exclusive with membership in other states. They view the political right to vote as linked to membership in a single political community. In addition, some U.S. citizens have raised the concern that dual Mexican citizenship will erode American citizenship and even U.S. sovereignty by weakening or dividing loyalty to the United States ("The Two Faces of Dual Nationality" 1998). Indeed, in discussing the dual citizenship law, some observers have even raised as a cultural fear the specter of the *Reconquista*, the Mexicans' reconquest of the American Southwest. That region became part of the United States through the 1848 Treaty of Guadalupe Hidalgo after the war with Mexico and through the Gadsen Purchase of 1853 (Aguayo 1998b; "The Two Faces" 1998).

In sum, the fear of potentially divided allegiances is also an important motive postponing the extension of political citizenship rights to Mexicans living abroad. Therefore, despite widespread support, this aspect of new political citizenship rights is still delayed.

OTHER, DIVERSE SOCIAL ACTORS' CONVERGENCE ON "DEMOCRATIZATION" (VARIOUSLY DEFINED)

In this chapter, I have shown how social actors including critical intellectuals, members and representatives of the unprivileged classes, the opposition press, and PRI moderates are converging on the secret ballot and the overall extension of the formal vote to previously unenfranchised groups of citizens, although they disagree radically about the substantive dimensions of citizenship.

Other Mexican social actors also agree on the desirability of the secret vote and on further Mexican democratization for a variety of additional, mutually contradictory reasons. For example, the representative of a leading Mexican business organization, CCE (Consejo Coordinador Empresarial), is convinced that paying the costs and taking the risks implied in a transition to democracy and party opening are preferable to remaining "trapped in a state of corruption at all levels which the monopolistic political model generated during its decades of governing the country" ("Preferible una costosa transicion" 1998:1). In this position, democratization is linked with the (eventual) achievement of juridic stability and security.

Independent labor-based nongovernmental organizations such as the *Centro de Studios del Movement Obrero y Socialista* (Center for Studies of the Socialist Workers' Movement) also support extension of the vote abroad (Ross Pineda 1999). Some labor union members have tried to use the climate of democratization to establish independent unions, thus strengthening workers' rights to political representation outside authoritarian corporate control (Green 1998; Botz 1995). Even the official corporatist unions under the aegis of the party-state have tried to evolve a "New Labor Culture" under democratization, in which the workers' constitutional right to labor justice is strengthened (Secretaría de Trabajo 1996:1). Indeed, the Supreme Court decision that unions have the right to choose their political affiliation—a practice that goes directly against the 51 years of corporatist syndicalism and forced political affiliation of unions to the PRI—is the most radical step toward breaking the party-state connection (*La Jornada* 1999).

Mexican archbishops have argued that the Church was "in favor of the secret, free, and reasoned vote" because it is a "liberty of expression" that allowed a citizen to vote for the candidate or party which best served his or her interests (No Clergy 1997:2). The pope, on his visit to Mexico, proclaimed that the Church is "always in favor of dialogue and pacific solutions to all conflicts" (including the Chiapas conflict), and that human rights should be respected (*Excelsior* January 13, 1999:1). The Church apparently has linked the greater exercise of political rights with respect for human rights and individual dignity.

Even editors of newspapers sympathetic to the official party-state government have recently spoken out in favor of democratization, applauding "the deepening of democracy [seen in] . . . the cleanness of recent elections, . . . opposition electoral advances at the state and municipal levels, . . . and the relations between the executive and legislative branches of government which had entered into a new manner of coordination and understanding, despite natural discrepancies" (*Excelsior* November 23, 1998a:1). Furthermore, the *Excelsior* editors believe that "civil society is fundamental to the understanding and solution to the problem of indigenous minorities" (*Excelsior* November 23, 1998). In fact, in a national survey conducted by the University of Guadalajara, over 80 percent of the members of civilians polled said that they did not believe that Indians enjoy the same rights as other Mexicans (Preston 1999:5). Why, then, given this agreement by multiple social groups on various aspects of democratization, has it been so difficult to define political citizenship rights regarding a group of citizens—the indigenous Mexicans —who often lack social and economic privilege?

THE ETHNIC DEMAND FOR JURIDIC RIGHTS TO POLITICAL AUTONOMY

The social demands of armed indigenous insurgents associated with the Zapatista Liberation Army (EZLN) also demonstrate the agreement, on formal law, of social actors with divergent substantive agendas. Two years after the armed uprising of the EZLN in January 1994, the EZLN and the Mexican federal government signed a series of formal agreements after attempting to resolve the conflict by negotiation (Camin 1997). These agreements include the February 1996 San Andrés Larrainzar Accords and, in November 1996, the Commission for Concord and Pacification (COCOPA) proposals created by the Mexican legislature.[11]

Although these concords are not yet formal law, they represent a clear formal rationalizing shift from the previous treatment of indigenous legal issues under the rubric of *usos y custumbres* (uses and customs) (Madrazo 1997:6). The term *usos y costumbres* refers broadly to a certain degree of informal tolerance for local indigenous customs and of traditional forms of local authority by Mexican authorities, inherited from the institutions and norms instituted by the Spanish Crown and the Catholic evangelists during the colonial period (Santibáñez and Gonzalo 1997:15–23; Stavenhagen 1995:12). Nevertheless, the Mexican state does not formally recognize legal pluralism based on the rights of indigenous peoples. Such state recognition already has been granted through autonomy statutes for indigenous regions within existing state boundaries in Nicaragua, Panama, and Brazil. These comparative Latin American cases may form a juridic precedent for the demands made by the EZLN (Díaz-Polanco 1991:206).[12]

In fact, a scholar of indigenous affairs, Hector Díaz-Polanco, argues that indigenous demands for self-governance in Latin America do not necessarily constitute a demand for political sovereignty and/or succession. Many Latin American indigenous groups may want only limited political autonomy within the existing state (Díaz-Polanco 1991:151–63, 166–70). Díaz-Polanco, however, believes that a new autonomous political-legal regime must be established to ensure indigenous political and other rights (1991:166). Furthermore, this regime must be assured by the highest legal guarantees—constitutional guarantees—and not merely by administrative guarantees, because the latter can be "annulled administratively." In contrast, constitutionally guaranteed autonomy ensures "liberty within law" (Díaz-Polanco 1991:166).

In Mexico, it appears that the EZLN is seeking formal law and its legal predictability or calculability precisely because it wishes to ensure juridic certainty at the highest constitutional levels for similar claims to political self-determination. The fundamental articles of the San Andrés Accords signed by the EZLN and the Mexican federal government include numerous constitutionally guaranteed rights such as the right to political autonomy, the right to self-determination for indigenous peoples, rights of territorial jurisdiction, and indigenous peoples' right to elect their internal government (EZLN *Reformas* 1996, Articles 1, 3, 5.1b., 5.12e/f). Many of these rights granted by the San Andrés Accords are designed to ensure indigenous actors' rights to political autonomy. They represent a departure from previous practice, especially the new social right of ensuring communities' economic viability through rights to collective ownership of land and property (EZLN *Reformas,* 1996:4, Proposal 13.2b, San Andrés Accords).

The San Andrés Accords of February 1996 possesses the status of an internal treaty in accordance with the juridic personalities of the federal government and the EZLN (Cepeda Neri 1999:36). In December 1996, in subsequent negotiations, further additions to the San Andrés Accords were made by the legislative pacification committee (COCOPA) and the EZLN; the COCOPA Accords were the result.

Yet despite this initial agreement on formal law by the EZLN and the Mexican federal government, broad substantive disagreement on the goals of the San Andrés-COCOPA Accords subsequently developed, and the negotiated effort to ensure peace broke down. Indeed, the convergence on process-oriented goals without agreement on content-oriented, substantively rational goals caused the Mexican government to balk at the legal ramifications of some aspects of the COCOPA Accords.

This divergence on substantive content is evident in the differing interpretations of the San Andrés-COCOPA Accords by the EZLN and the federal government. The EZLN apparently understood the San Andrés-COCOPA agreements as a strategy of formal law, pursued to ensure the content-oriented ethical maximization of social justice. This point explains why the EZLN linked the political right to choose autonomous self-governance with the right to ethnocultural freedom, with democracy, and with a state of law (EZLN Foro Especial Transicion a la Democracia, 1994, Mesa 3). Furthermore, the EZLN demanded the right to collective ownership of land and property to ensure the economic viability of its communities (EZLN *Reformas* 1996:4, Proposal 13.2b, San Andrés Accords). Official government statistics show that indigenous groups in many Mexican states do not possess the same social rights, on average, as do nonindigenous Mexican nationals (National Indigenous Institute 1995:Table 1).

The maximization of social justice follows from the EZLN's vision of democracy as "implying a new culture and a new relationship between the governed and the governing, and new forms of social living together" (EZLN Transición a la Democracia 1994, Mesa 3:1). Neither electoral democracy alone nor representative democracy based on elections "is sufficient" for Mexico, although the "Mexican transition to democracy should necessarily pass through clean and transparent elections" (EZLN Transición a la Democracia 1994, Mesa 3:2). Rather, the EZLN believes that the Mexican transition to democracy requires "the dismantling of all of the legal and metalegal entanglements that make up the party-state regime, [and] the recovery, for Mexicans, of the right to determine the political economy, new forms of participation, and direct control over public life" (EZLN Transición a la Democracia 1994, Mesa 3:2).

Comparative citizenship scholar Will Kymlicka (1998:178–79) notes that claims to self-government by social actors in a nation-state are often perceived by the governing authorities as weakening the bonds of the larger political community and even as questioning its authority and permanence. This occurs because the basic claim underlying self-governing rights is not simply that some groups are disadvantaged within the political community (as reflected in representation rights), nor that the political community is culturally diverse (as reflected in polyethnic rights). Instead the claim implies that there is more than one political community, and that the authority of the larger state cannot be assumed to take precedence over that of the constituent national communities. "If democracy is the rule of 'the people,' national minorities claim that there is more than one people, each with the right to rule itself" (Kymlicka 1998:175).[13]

The Mexican government fears the EZLN demands for self-government as steps on the road to secession; this is evident in each of the government's subsequent observations, interpretations, and critiques of the COCOPA's legal initiatives. For example, the federal government claims that when the COCOPA proposals speak of autonomy for indigenous peoples "as part of the Mexican state," they are unclear about the boundaries of that autonomy (Presidencia 1998a:2). It claims that the COCOPA proposals create "special" legal regimes for indigenous peoples in matters of communication laws and education policy, which would stand outside the existing Mexican Constitution (Presidencia 1998a:2–8). One constitutional scholar sympathetic to the federal government argues that the 1996 COCOPA proposal for indigenous-based collective property rights even violates the Mexican Constitution because it implies removal of the existing *ejidal* property rights of *ejidatarios*, indigenous persons, and peasants (Montes 1999). Government officials contend that such changes to property rights would generate land battles throughout Mexico and would create a "grave social problem" (Presidencia 1998a; Preston 1999:5).

Perhaps most controversial is the struggle over rights to indigenous municipal autonomy. Since 1994 the EZLN has taken over a number of municipal governments in Chiapas and has declared them "autonomous" self-governed political entities controlled by the EZLN (Dillon 1999; Presidencia 1998b). The federal government, in turn, has attempted to "remunicipalize" Chiapas: that is, to reclaim these municipalities and to create new ones (Victorio 1999).

In this political context, the federal government claims that the right of self-determination for Mexican indigenous peoples "as an absolute right stands outside the framework of the existing Article 4 of the Mexican Constitution" (Presidencia 1998b:8). To grant this right would "establish a fourth level of government" (Presidencia 1998b:8). According to the federal government, the COCOPA proposal's concept of "municipalities that belong to indigenous peoples" is also anti-constitutional because a municipality cannot recognize an entity other than the federal entity of which it forms a part, as established by Constitutional Article 115 (Presidencia 1998b:8).

THE FAILURE OF CONVERGENCE

It appears that the Mexican federal government initially signed the formal San Andrés Accords to achieve distinctive content-oriented goals, especially to maintain the Chiapas conflict within the boundaries of negotiation and agreement (Camin 1997:3; Presidencia 1995). Nevertheless, government officials and legal professionals sympathetic to the government have adopted strategies whose results maintain the continuity and predictability of modern law and administration, particularly with respect to municipal autonomy. The existing Mexican constitution undergoes fewer changes as a result of the federal government's position rather than that of the EZLN's. This failure to agree on formal law shows how formally rational accords in fact are compromised by the substantive demands of justice.

Since the breakdown of the September 1996 accords, both sides have pursued alternative content-oriented strategies in an attempt to mobilize public support for their positions. As a result of its 1998 nationwide referendum, the federal government has created an alternative "Law Initiative Regarding Rights and Indigenous Culture" and has submitted it to the Mexican Congress for consideration. The federal government claims that this legal initiative conforms to the original San Andrés Accords (*Excelsior* 1999c). Significantly, the new initiative does not legally recognize indigenous social actors as a separate "people" (*pueblo*) distinct from the Mexican nation as a whole (Presidencia 1998b:Article 4). Such formal constitutional recognition of indigenous persons has been a long-standing demand of some indigenous Mexicans (Díaz-Polanco 1991:203–4). The EZLN set forth its own referendum in 1999, called "The Rights of Indian Peoples and the End to the War of Extermination." One of the key purposes of this referendum was to revive public support for the 1996 San Andrés-COCOPA Accords (Garrido 1999).

In the context of existing civil rights and territorial-political divisions, it has not yet proved possible to formalize new rights to indigenous self-government and the attendant rights to collective property. This is the case in part because even at the level of constitutional interpretation, there are disagreements about what is at stake in the juridification of indigenous groups' rights to collective property and to political self-determination. Scholars of indigenous issues, whether or not they are sympathetic to the EZLN's cause, apparently agree that formal juridification of the rights of self-government in fact implies significant changes to the Mexican constitution. Díaz-Polanco (1991:206) argues that even the juridic recognition of local-level indigenous authorities and entities (such as the Council of Elders and the Assembly) violates Constitutional Article 115, which establishes that "there will be no intermediate authority" between the municipality and the state government.

Others who are sympathetic to the EZLN's cause, however, minimize the impact of the COCOPA Accords. They argue that indigenous groups already possess the informal capacity to satisfy their claims for collective land under the mechanism of "recognition and entitlement of common goods" (Montes 1999:1). According to this interpretation, allowing municipalities to recognize that they belong to an indigenous people does not signify the juridification of an intermediate (indigenous) authority superior to the municipality. It merely implies the "strengthening of the sense of identity of the same municipalities, giving a real and efficient basis to the free association of municipalities and the coordination of their communal activities," and is consistent with constitutional Article 115, Section 3 (Montes

1999:1). Thus the social actors' inability to agree on an adjudicated acceptance of EZLN's claims to self-government is reflected in the conflicting constitutional interpretations.

The COCOPA, led by a group of opposition legislators on the left, has been attempting to revive dialogue in search of a peaceful solution to the conflict in Chiapas (Beceríl 1999). Some of its members claim that both the EZLN and the federal government have adopted "irreducible positions" that do not advance a social agreement on a resolution (leader of the COCOPA and federal PRD legislator Carlos Morales Vazquez, *Proceso* 1999:14; Siempre 1999). Thus, despite the social actors' initial formal agreement as expressed in the San Andrés-COCOPA Accords, they have not yet provided a scaffolding for granting more substantive citizenship rights.

IMPLICATIONS

The sociological study of the extension of political rights in Mexico is an important dimension of the study of democratization in third wave transitions to democracy. Democracy, after all, is a multidimensional set of structures (Collins 1998:19; Geddes 1999; O'Donnell 1996:37; Therborn 1990:4). Political rights represent central cultural expressions and crystallizations of struggle.

I have shown here that the extension of political citizenship rights is a process subject to the dialectic of formal and substantive rationalization. On one hand, this process takes the form of "ethical maximization of social justice." In the Mexican case this includes pressures, by intellectuals and by members of the unprivileged groups, for the free exercise and extension of the franchise, and for indigenous rights to political self-determination. On the other hand, the struggle over political citizenship rights in Mexico takes the form of "ethical minimization," in which government officials, legal professionals, and some intellectuals advocate policies leading to continuity and predictability in modern law and administration.

The Mexican case also shows that these two dialectical modes of applying the law (content- and process-oriented) and the attendant strategies represent a recurrent social conflict in various related arenas of the struggle for democratization. Democratization, as an emergent form of political authority, accelerates when multiple social actors with different motives (possessing simultaneous ethical, political, utilitarian, and instrumental dimensions) are able to agree. In this case, I have shown how attempts at convergence have occurred in four related empirical dimensions of political rights: (1) the freer exercise of the secret ballot, (2) the evolution of the secret ballot in intraparty elections, (3) the extension of the franchise abroad, and (4) the juridification of indigenous groups' rights to self-government.

Such formal convergence may or may not provide a framework for granting more substantive citizenship rights. In the case of the secret ballot in intraparty elections, the efforts of multiple social actors, including civic groups and moderate PRI members, apparently have enlarged the exercise of existing franchise rights. Mexico's electoral institutions have ensured increasing competitiveness through the 1990s, and violations of suffrage rights increasingly are prosecuted by governmental institutions (Aguayo 1998a).

Yet, efforts to extend the franchise abroad and to formally ensure rights to autonomous self-government have not proved successful. Some key members of the party-state perceive these new political rights as pathbreaking, and view them as potential and actual threats to the political interests of the PRI and to the territorial integrity of the current nation. These perceptions delay further movement to extend political citizenship rights to Mexicans living abroad. The failure to reach agreement on the San Andrés-COCOPA Accords highlights the difficulty of formalizing new rights to indigenous self-government and the attendant social rights to collective property in the context of existing civil rights and territorial-political divisions.

Mexico's delayed transition to democracy is an important case lying outside the Anglo-centric narrative on the extension of political rights. In the late twentieth century, delayed transitions to democracy have been characterized by lengthy social struggles over political rights. In 1985, early in the transition in Kenya, the Catholic Church spoke out against the elimination of the secret ballot in primary elections, as well as against social injustice, nepotism, and ethnic favoritism (Barkan 1994:57). In a direct parallel with the Mexican Civic Alliance movement, the Church in Kenya also studied electoral fraud and provided detailed documentation of widespread rigging, bribery, intimidation, and coercion in the 1988 parliamentary elections (Barkan 1994:57).

In Taiwan's delayed transition to democracy, the political opposition began as a movement for greater political rights and for democratic procedures including the secret ballot (Cheng 1989:485). As in Mexico, the Taiwanese party-state regime responded to societal demands for democratization with a slow, extended process of political liberalization, and with the expansion of intraparty competition.

In Tanzania, as in Mexico, labor unions tried to break away from the confines of the single party and its official unionism. They pressed for independent political rights to representation by creating a new, independent confederation of trade unions (Chege 1994:65). Similarly, in Tanzania, the party-state was willing to concede more autonomy to labor but would not countenance independent trade unions with wage-bargaining rights (Botz 1995; Chege 1994:65).

The analysis in this chapter suggests that in delayed transitions to democracy, the process differs from the Anglo sequence (the extension of civil, political, and then social rights) in at least one important way. The Mexican case suggests that the free exercise and the further extension of political rights predominate. To be sure, improved access to justice, guarantees for existing civil rights, and improved social rights are important components of democratization. Nevertheless, when social rights emerge as a significant component of the democratizing struggle, as in EZLN demands for collective property rights or in independent unions' demands for wage-bargaining rights, they arise as social demands for political rights to autonomous political organizations and self-governance. Thus the struggle to extend *political* rights is a central feature of delayed transitions to democracy.

This social demand for greater political rights reflects the fusion of party and state that characterizes the authoritarian state, and represents social actors' desire to loosen or even break that institutional connection. From a sociological standpoint, in third wave democratization, social actors' attempts both to preserve and to dissolve the party-state fusion will remain subject to multiple tensions between process- and content-oriented strategies. Democratization accelerates the search for formal legal grounds for substantive citizenship rights. When multiple social actors with differing motives can agree on the extension of those formal political rights, such guarantees may provide the support.

Nevertheless, we must expect continuous process and flux, rather than a finished product, in the demands of these social actors. Such a process is demonstrated in opposition parties' recent efforts to change laws to facilitate the development of coalition candidates (*Proceso* 1999), in the fielding of joint PAN-PRD candidates in local races as a new party tactic to overturn the old regime, and in the nascent commitment of opposition parties to field a joint presidential candidate.

NOTES

1. More than 500 PRD militants have died in political violence since 1988 (PRD 1996).

2. This general argument is related to the idea that social action may be oriented in four ideal-typical ways: instrumentally rational, value-rational, affectual, and traditional. In any concrete case, the "orientation of action to an order involves a wide variety of motives" (Weber 1978:31).

3. Lear McConnell (1996) found that 34 percent of a random sample of members of the Civic Alliance National Assembly had previously participated in civic and human rights groups. Most frequently specified were Amnesty International, the Southern California Human Rights Center, Ceddhac, IMDEC, Mexico's Civic Movement, CICAS, the San Luis Potosi Civic Front, the Sinaloa Civic Front, CODEHUTAR, the Civic Front for Families, and GRAPPA.

4. These figures must be interpreted in comparison with national averages. According to 1990 data, 9.2 percent of the over-25 age group had postsecondary education, 23.4 percent had some high school education, 19.9 percent had completed primary school, 28.6 percent had not completed primary school, and 18.8 percent had no schooling (*Statistical Abstract of Latin America* 1995:244).

5. Aguayo's discourse also illustrates the importance of liberty, autonomy, and activity, characteristic of the symbolism of democratic codes of civil society (Alexander and Smith 1993).

6. Since the 1994 Mexican presidential election, further party-state legal reforms in the administration of electoral justice have given more autonomy in official decision-making to nonpartisan affiliated law professors, lawyers, and legal theorists in conjunction with the demands of opposition political parties (Becerra 1997). Nevertheless, until 1998–99 the party-state retained fundamental administrative control over the juridic checking of elections, the disbursement of party funds for campaigns, and the juridic processing of claims of electoral violations, and the PRI received a disproportionate share of public campaign resources ("Although" 1996). Under the November 1996 law, registered civic movements

now have the option of establishing alliances to run candidates for popular election, although limitations on funds for coalition candidates remain (*La Jornada* 1997b).

7. Similarly, the effort to increase Mexican politicians' accountability to citizens as a substantively ethical/political goal has led to *formal rationalizing* consequences that conflict with continued party-state political control. For example, the Civic Alliance leaders' successful petition to the Mexican presidency for accurate public information on the organization of the executive branch, its budget, and the president's salary increased the formally rational reach of the law by extending the application of constitutional Article 8 (a citizen's right to petition) to the office of the presidency (Alianza Cívica 1996). The presidency's response in accordance with the law also marks the production of a tangible, written formal document that answers questions about executive affairs previously protected by administrative secrecy (Monasterio 1996).

8. For a response by the head of the electoral justice tribunal to these criticisms from democratizing actors, see de la Peza (1997).

9. The issue of the vote abroad for Mexican migrants emerged previously, in the Vasconcellist presidential campaigns of 1929 (*Factor Tiempo* 1999).

10. Mexican immigrants send an estimated U.S.$6 billion home each year ("Expatriate Mexicans" 1998).

11. For an analysis of the military dimensions and controversies of the conflict between EZLN and the Mexican government during this period, see (Ballesteros Corona and Cunningham 1998; Harvey 1994; Nash 1995; Rich 1997). In addition to the legal negotiations, which are discussed later, each social actor has maintained the right to use arms against the other. The federal government keeps a strong army presence in the state of Chiapas, while the EZLN is still an armed insurgency force.

12. Rather, it recognizes the multicultural composition of the Mexican nation, "sustained originally by its indigenous peoples," and promises to "protect and promote the development of indigenous languages, cultures, uses, customs, resources, and specific forms of social organization and to guarantee its integrants effective access to the jurisdiction of the State" (Article 4, Arco 1995:7).

13. This represents a growing tendency toward regionalism and the recognition of distinctive regions by the central state, which fragments existing nations and nationalities into distinct ethnicities and cultural subunits (Soysal 1998:210). In France, this has occurred with the Bretons, Corsicans, Basques, and Occitans; in Britain, with the Scots and the Welsh; in Italy, with the Lombards and the Sardinians. In Spain, the central government increasingly accommodates autonomous entities and provides for regional languages.

Chapter 5

The Delayed Transitions Model in Comparative Perspective

The analysis in this book reveals novel sociological patterns of democratization social action including the dual sociocultural mobilization of classes and political parties, and the continual ongoing social struggle over the extension of political rights characteristic of delayed transitions to democracy. This social pattern appears to differ from both the social class bases posited from the Western European democratizing experience ("middle-class thesis," the "working-class thesis," and the "working-class/middle-class alliance thesis") and the Anglo-based theories of the sequential extension of citizenship rights (civil, political, social).

Instead, I have argued in this book, the authoritarian corporate organization of interests, forms of political consciousness, state-civil society relations and political institutions, has delayed Mexico's transition to democracy by: (1) inhibiting the development of an independent, anti-authoritarian working class consciousness and by creating a state-dependent middle class; (2) historically mediating demands for political participation stemming from socioeconomic development process through a regime-sponsored political pluralism that has divided the political opposition and caused the dual, but nonpolitically allied mobilization of sectors of the anti-authoritarian middleclasses/nonprivileged class with distinctive interests, political and economic values; and, (3) creating a continual, ongoing democratizing struggle over the extension of political rights linked to the effort to disperse power in collective decision-making bodies (legislatures, independent judiciaries, electoral bodies, federalism).

The analysis here thus raises the comparative question of whether such social patterns exist in other the cases of delayed transitions and suggests analytic directions for future research on this question. More specifically, the delayed transitions model identified in this book suggests two sets of sociological factors particularly crucial for understanding gradual transitions to democracy: (1) political divisions between the opposition parties and the old single party by the urban, educated, well-to-do voters and (2) the intertwining of a general desire for democratic government with continued public support for the old single party into the new phase of competitive elections.

To demonstrate that these factors are not unique to Mexico, I extend the delayed transitions model to Taiwan, and (briefly) to Tanzania. Both Taiwan and Tanzania possess several features in common with Mexico: both are governed by non-Leninist corporate authoritarian regimes in which the major institutions of society historically were subordinated to dominant-party control (Barkan 1994: Chege 1994; Chu 1996); both possessed strong executives with metaconstitutional ruling powers; and rulers in both nations legitimated their rule with a strategy of "tutelary democracy" based on semicompetitive elections and limited political pluralism (Collier 1982:127–28; King 1993).

In Taiwan's and Tanzania's transitions to competitive elections in the 1990s, the delayed transitions model predicts (1) that the urban, educated, well-to-do voters are divided politically three ways, favoring the single party and divided between the two anti-authoritarian opposition parties; and (2) that multiparty democracy emerges from a strategy of "tutelary democracy" in which the old single party will continue to enjoy electoral and popular legitimacy among significant sectors of the nonprivileged electorate. This continued widespread viability of the old single party in both Taiwan and Tanzania, combined with the citizens' general desire for a democratic government, results in a slow, delayed transition to democracy.

A POLITICALLY DIVIDED URBAN, EDUCATED, WELL-TO-DO ELECTORATE: TAIWAN

Historically the Taiwanese single-party regime—the Kuomintang or KMT— was an exclusionary, non-Leninist regime resting on an ethnic bifurcation. The KMT restricted peasants from political participation in China; after its removal to Taiwan, it adopted an exclusionary policy toward islander Chinese living in Taiwan (King 1993:146). This bifurcation of ethnic mainlanders and islanders and the exclusion of the latter from political participation softened after 1977, when KMT elites initiated liberalization and democratization in response to demands for the "Taiwanization" of institutional and political life. Thus the KMT regime was a single-party system with ethnic dualities, but did not rest on a racial base (Huntington 1970:16) after democratization began.

The 1992 Legislative Yuan election gave birth to the first democratically elected national legislature in Taiwan's history (Chu 1996:455). The 1994 Legislative Yuan election represents a further opportunity to examine how social cleavages became linked to political cleavages in the series of competitive legislative elections in Taiwan throughout the 1990s.

The social analysis of voter alignments in the 1992 Legislature Yuan election[1] reflects the early entanglement of democratic reform with the issue of national independence from China. Table 5.1 shows that the opposition-party vote for the Democratic Progressive Party (DPP) is explained by "nonethnic mainlander" ethnic identification and by the desire for political independence from China.[2] The DPP emerged as a faction that split off from the KMT in 1986 and made independence from China a central part of its platform (Chu 1996). In sociological terms, the DPP constituency represents a demand for further social inclusion of nonmainlander ethnic Taiwanese.

The social analysis of the 1992 Legislative Yuan election also reveals support for statism and for the statist policies of the KMT regime in two ways (see Table 5.2). First, as in Mexico, the core social constituency of the single party consists of civil servants: that is, the statist middle classes. The 1992 KMT vote is also explained by support from ethnic mainlanders; this fact reflects the historical linkage of ethnic mainlanders and their descendants with the party-state regime. Thus the social support for the Taiwanese single party in 1992 was based strongly on a coalition of civil servants and other regime loyalists (ethnic mainlanders).

Second, support for authoritarian statism is evident in the generalized support for the KMT regime in the early 1990s. A series of questions on political culture included in the 1992 Taiwanese General Social Change Survey reveals that 53 percent of the respondents said they "liked" the KMT, but only 23 percent reported "liking" the opposition DPP party. This suggests that the DPP opposition arose in a sociopolitical climate still strongly favoring the single-party regime. At the same time, however, only 14 percent ($N = 173$) of these respondents thought democracy was not suitable for Taiwan when asked whether they agreed with the statement, "So long as the government is efficient in maintaining social order and solving traffic and economic problems, whether our country is democratic or not is not very important" ("Taiwanese General Social Change Survey" 1992:43). Fully 86 percent of the respondents ($N = 1,042$) did not agree with the idea that government needed only to take care of law and social order without attending to issues of multiparty-ism. In other words, the Taiwanese respondents expressed general support for the idea of "democracy," but at the same time preferred the single-party KMT regime to the rising opposition DPP party.

After the 1992 election, the issue of democratic reform no longer occupied center stage as democratization accelerated the KMT's inclusion of ethnic Taiwanese in the ranks of the KMT. As a result, subethnicity and national identity were displaced as sources of a central democratizing cleavage (Chu 1996). By the time of the 1994 legislative elections, socioeconomic affairs had displaced ethnic divisions as important issues.

The rise in the importance of socioeconomic issues in Taiwan's delayed transition to democracy is also the result of the emergence of a second opposition party—the New Party (NP). Just as the DPP had emerged from the KMT in 1986, so the NP split off from the dominant KMT regime. In 1994 the NP emerged to run in the Legislative Yuan elections on an anti-corruption, pro-social justice platform (Chu 1996:477). The social analysis of voter alignments in the 1994 elections reveals significant divisions in the support of educated, well-to-do voters for the

Table 5.1
The Social Bases of Voter Alignments in Taiwanese Legislative Yuan Elections, 1992 and 1994

| | 1992 Legislative Yuan Elections | | 1994 Legislative Yuan Elections | | |
	KMT (n=703)	DPP (n=705)	KMT (n=1096)	DPP (n=571)	NP (n=218)
Urban	-0.6408	0.2794	-0.0040*	0.0001*	0.8106
Education	-0.6651	-0.7876	-0.0000*	0.0264*	0.0000*
Income	----	——	0.3404	-0.5700	-0.5476
Age	-0.0795	0.5481	0.1587	-0.0336*	-0.6396
Gov't	0.0390*	0.8011	0.2683	-0.7894	0.9370
Ethnic Main	0.0000*	-0.0014*	-0.0000*	-0.0001*	0.0000*
Independence	-0.0000*	0.0000*	----	----	----

Table 5.2
Split Middle-Class Vote in Taiwan, 1992 and 1994

| | 1992 Legislative Yuan Elections (n=1037) | | | 1994 Legislative Yuan Elections (n=2,766) | | |
	Education	Income	Urban (Taipei/Non-Taipei)	Education	Income	Urban (Taipei/Non-Taipei)
KMT	84.6%	83.6%	84.9%/83.9%	66.4%	68.2%	53.4%/72.5%
DPP	15.3%	16.4%	15.1%/16.1%	12.3%	12.1%	19.3%/11.1%
NP	n/a	n/a	n/a	21.1%	19.5%	27.4%/16.4%

Includes education categories of secondary, university and above; income categories of medium (below $20,000) and high (above $20,000); urban was divided into Taipei (capital city) versus non-Taipei.

two opposition parties. Both the DPP vote and the NP vote are explained by the votes of the more highly educated electorate. The urban, educated, young voters supported the DPP; the highly educated, ethnic mainlanders supported the NP. In contrast, by 1994, the core social base of the dominant KMT (government workers and ethnic mainlanders) had shifted significantly to the rural, uneducated electorate.

As in Mexico, the Taiwanese policy of limited political pluralism and semicompetitive elections created a triadic party structure in which the dominant single party competed with two politically divided opposition parties, one of which stressed issues of socioeconomic justice. Similarly, as in Mexico, the Taiwanese results show that economic development and democracy are related positively and that this relationship is carried by the anti-authoritarian middle classes, as theories of the Western European democratizing experience suggest. Significant sectors of the middle classes, however, still strongly support the authoritarian regime. Thus the middle classes are deeply divided politically. Table 5.2 shows that significant sectors of the middle classes continue to support the dominant party in both the 1992 and the 1994 elections. Such political divisions in the social alignments of urban, educated, well-to-do Taiwanese voters, combined with other factors such as international tensions with China (Chu 1996), contributed to the KMT victory in the 1996 presidential elections.

TUTELARY DEMOCRACY AND THE CONTINUED POPULARITY OF THE SINGLE PARTY INTO THE COMPETITIVE PHASE OF ELECTIONS: TANZANIA

The delayed transitions model also predicts that a strategy of tutelary democracy is an important cause of the emergence of multipartyism at the mass level, in which the old single party manages and organizes the transition to increasingly competitive elections. In Tanzania, as in Mexico, most of the major institutions of society (the press, labor unions, farmers' cooperatives, businesses, and the National Assembly) were brought under single-party control in the consolidation of the authoritarian regime (Barkan 1994; Chege 1994). Although Tanzanian regime elites relied on a more intensive statist policy based on collective farms and modeled on the Soviet farms (*ujamaa* or familyhood), rulers also used mass nationalization as a socializing value. Many citizens believed in these values in both Tanzania and Mexico (Africa Confidential 1997:3; Bartra 1989:56–57).

In Tanzania, executive elites allowed semipolitical pluralism in the form of extensive electoral competition within the dominant party (the CCM), whereby the electorate could vote for only one presidential candidate but could choose between candidates from the same party for each parliamentary constituency (Cliffe 1967). The rate of elite turnover in parliament due to voters' choice was comparatively high (Barkan 1994); analysts categorized Tanzania's system as a competitive one-party system in which "voters seemed sufficiently attracted by the available choices to sustain genuine turnout figures at relatively high levels" (Bratton and van de Walle 1997:80).

In 1991, after the severe economic crises of the 1980s,[3] Tanzanian dominant party (CCM) elites introduced a multiparty system of competitive elections in the context of a divided opposition. At that time, however, only 21.5 percent of Tanzanians surveyed favored a multiparty system; 77.2 percent still favored a single-party system (Presidential Commission Report 1992). In 1994, 36 percent preferred a multiparty democracy, while 55 percent favored the single-party system (REDET Baseline Survey Report 1997). In 1994, 53 percent of Tanzanians surveyed still believed that the government party (CCM) greatly protected the national interest (Killian 1998:26).

The CCM dominated the 1995 presidential election and the legislative by-elections of 1996–99 (Africa Confidential 1997:3). By 1996, the proportion of Tanzanian citizens surveyed who supported a multiparty system had grown to 49.5 percent; 42 percent still favored the single-party system (REDET Baseline Survey Report 1997).

The evolution of mass beliefs favoring multiparty elections throughout the 1990s, in the context of the CCM's continued electoral hegemony, offers comparative evidence for the continued legacy of the strategy in which rulers are legitimated by tutelary democracy controlled from above. Tanzanian elites introduced multiparty competition, although there was little evidence of widespread support for the idea. At the same time, the incumbent leadership has repeatedly sent the message, especially during electoral campaigns, that opposition parties tend to elicit conflicts like those in Rwanda and Burundi (Killian 1998). In some of his public speeches, Julius Nyerere, former president and the architect of the single-party system, even discouraged the electorate from voting for opposition parties, saying "a vote for the opposition is a vote for violence and national disintegration" (IFES Report 1995:4). This position, too, is paralleled in Mexico among incumbent regime elites: In the 1994 presidential election, the leftist opposition party was more likely to be portrayed on the government-controlled television as dangerous and violent than was the governing party or the rightist opposition party (Acosta and Rosales 1995).

The Mexican case also shows parallels to the Tanzanian citizens' favorable opinion of the CCM in 1994 despite 25 years of economic deterioration. Kaufman and Zuckerman (1998:369) argue that support for the PRI's neoliberal economic reforms, found in 53 percent of the population, remained surprisingly strong in view of the extraordinary economic hardships most Mexicans have endured since 1995. Again, the weakness of the political opposition parties is an important part of the explanation. Although a large number of opposition parties registered to compete in Tanzania's elections in 1995, they failed failure to forge a united opposition alliance. This failure illustrates the "success of the CCM at limiting the ability of society to mobilize nationally" (Costello 1996:145). In the words of Julius Nyerere's son, an opposition member of parliament, "Opposition politics in Tanzania means everybody for himself and God for us all. . . . Unity can only come after fighting it out" (Africa Confidential 1997:3).

Although these comparisons between Taiwan, Tanzania, and Mexico have been brief, it is clear that the factors identified to explain Mexico also apply to delayed transitions to democracy elsewhere. In Taiwan, despite the rise of an anti-authoritarian middle class, significant middle-class support for the KMT regime continues. The case of Tanzania reveals how multipartyism emerges from a strategy of tutelary democracy, in which the old single-party regime is an important shaper of mass beliefs. In both Taiwan and Tanzania, the old single party is still capable of shaping and limiting the mobilization of society.

CONCLUSION

Mexico's delayed transition to democracy suggests a comparative conclusion. Unlike the breakdown of military regimes, where former dictators' political organizations do not play as significant a role, the single party remains central in the transition to competitive politics. Delayed transitions to democracy are characterized by the gradual reconfiguration of the cultural bases of legitimation, as opposed to a sharp break in the legitimacy formula of military regimes and a "pacted" transition to competitive elections. Delayed transitions include no "first" competitive election, as discussed extensively in the literature on the breakdown of military regimes (Gunther et al. 1996; Linz 1990; Shin 1994; Schmitter and Karl 1994). Instead a series of increasingly competitive elections is held, in which mass actors wax and wane in their electoral support for the opposition. The outcome of these elections depends to a large extent on a variety of factors, including opposition parties' mobilization strategies, the relative economic fortunes of the regime, the relative freedom of the media, and (not least) the relative fairness of the electoral rules of engagement.

Thus, to understand the pattern of delayed transitions to democracy, one must analyze the social sources of delay. Accounts that rely on the power of transformative industrialism are modeled too closely on the Western European democratizing experience to fully explain the social structural dynamics of these delayed transitions. In Western Europe, social transformations—the national revolution and the industrial revolution—produced various social divisions, which then became linked to four modern political cleavages (center-periphery, church-state, land-industry, worker-capitalist) (Lipset and Rokkan [1967] 1985). In non-Leninist single-party regimes, however, delayed transitions reflect the corporate structure of interests and the forms of political consciousness that characterize such regimes. Economic development and even the evolution of democracy were thought to be managed most successfully, at least initially, under the tutelage of a single-party regime. Twentieth-century democratic Western European party systems are based on the party divisions and on citizens' voting behavior; these, in turn, reflect the historical development of the four central political cleavages, especially the land-industry and worker-capitalist divisions.

Instead, the social analysis of voter alignments indicates a social pattern in which the corporate shaping of interests and the forms of political consciousness of citizens in modern authoritarian states still influence the linkage of social cleavages to party structures, even in competitive elections. As shown in the cases of Mexico and Taiwan, the continued support of important sectors of the middle classes for the old single party suggests support for statism and statist policies characteristic of a state-dependent authoritarian corporate middle class. The political divisions within the anti-authoritarian middle classes also appear to differ from the sociopolitical cleavages of the class/mass parties of Western European industrialized nations. There, the land/industry-rural/urban social cleavage historically translated into a political conflict between conservatives (landed interests) and liberals (the rising class of urban industrial entrepreneurs) (Lipset and Rokkan [1967] 1985:134). In Mexico, businessmen's votes are divided between the anti-authoritarian rightist opposition party and the technocratic factions controlling the statist-turned-neoliberal single-party regime.

This pattern of division in urban, educated opposition also reflects the corporate organization of forms of political consciousness, in which the single-party regime rejects dogmatic ideology in favor of broad "catch-all" appeals to progress, development, and the nation. Strongly organized ideological opposition is difficult in such a diffuse, adaptive, pragmatic environment: Statism can be abandoned by regime elites in favor of neoliberalism, as occurred in Mexico and in Tanzania, and ethnic exclusionism can be converted into ethnic inclusionism, as occurred in Taiwan. The case of Mexico reveals that ideological appeals associated with the "worker-capitalist" conflict emerge in the form of the distinctive "pro-statist" and "anti-statist" economic values of opposition parties' supporters. On the whole, however, in delayed transitions to democracy, the middle classes are a fluctuating, internally complex social force whose preferences cannot easily be theorized as predominantly anti-authoritarian.

Finally, the continued popular legitimation of the old single party, even in the face of economic crises and its eventual electoral retreat to the nonprivileged sectors of the electorate (as in Mexico and Taiwan), also reflects the legacy of the corporate organization of interests and forms of political consciousness. The single party's historical efforts to redistribute land to peasants (as in Mexico and Tanzania), its rhetorical stress on social justice and equality, and even the corporate authoritarian structuring of organized labor have left a legacy of support for the regime among the nonprivileged. This corporate legacy also discourages the emergence of a strong anti-authoritarian working class on the ideological left, which is hypothesized as the central actor in the Western European democratizing experience (Rueschmeyer et al. 1992).

The social alignments of the breakdown of such populist, non-Leninist, authoritarian single-party systems reflect a corporate organization of interests and forms of political consciousness that may well represent a new type of democracy. The case of Botswana's "paternalist democracy" suggests that the electoral dominance of Botswana's single party after 30 years of fair and free elections is related to the continued "paternalistic" ties between urban government leaders and their rural subordinates (Holm 1988; Molutsi and Holm 1989:282). If the case of Botswana is a harbinger of the future, the democracies that emerge from delayed transitions may well be broad-based, populist, and quite possibly paternalist.

NOTES

1. Data analyzed in this chapter were collected in the research project "Taiwanese General Social Change Survey," sponsored by the National Science Council, Republic of China. This project was conducted by the Sun Yat-Sen Institute of Social Sciences and Philosophy of Academica Sinica, Taipei, Taiwan, and was directed by Drs. Chium Hei-Yuan, Ying-hwa, and Chang. The Office of Survey Research of the Academica Sinica is responsible for the data distributed. I appreciate these institutes' and individuals' assistance in providing the data; the views expressed here are my own.

2. The following variables are included in the model: urban (Taipei/non-Taipei), education, income, age, mainlander ethnicity, civil service occupation and pro- or anti-DPP independence. The polls consist of 2,722 personal interviews conducted four months before the 1992 Legislative Yuan election and the 1994 Legislative Yuan election. The sampling frame of the 1992 survey followed a multistage area of probability design. Through a series of steps, the survey designers selected cities, counties, districts, townships/villages, and precincts with probabilities proportionate to their population of adults between ages 20 and 64. I used standard logistic regression analysis in the data analysis.

3. In the late 1960s and 1970s Tanzania relied on a policy of state-controlled economic development. In the mid-1970s and 1980s, severe economic crises became manifest in declining levels of foreign reserves, negative per capita growth rates, budgetary and balance of payment crises, the deterioration of basic social services such as education, health, and water, and poor living standards (Barkan 1994). Government programs became severely underfunded; by the mid-1980s, the government could no longer maintain its legitimacy by providing free social services to the public (Chege 1994). The CCM began a series of responses to IMF conditions in the mid-1980s; these culminated in 1995, when it began to move toward a market economy through privatization of the state, more foreign investment, increased tourism, and reductions in the number of civil servants (Costello 1996).

Bibliography

"A un Paso de la Unidad." 1976. *Triunfo*, September 25, pp. 9–10.

Abel, Richard L. 1988. "Lawyers in the Civil World," pp. 1–43. In *Lawyers in Society, Vol. 2: The Civil Law World*, edited by Richard L. Abel and Philip S.C. Lewis. Berkeley: University of California Press.

Abel, Richard L. and Philip S.C. Lewis 1995. "Putting Law Back into the Sociology of Lawyers," pp. 281–330. In *Lawyers in Society: An Overview*, edited by Richard L. Abel and Philip S.C. Lewis. Berkeley: University of California Press.

"Absentee Vote Proposal Draws Fire on Both Side of the Border." 1999. *The Mexico City News* (February 2).

Acosta, Valverte and Parra Rosales. 1995. "Civic Alliance Report on Mexican News Coverage." Mexico City: Civic Alliance.

Africa Confidential. 1997. December 19, 1997, Vol. 38, No. 25; April 1997, Vol. 38, No. 8; December 1996, Vol. 37, No. 21.

Aguayo, Sergio. 1995. "A Mexican Milestone, Field Reports." *Journal of Democracy*, 6(2): 157–68.

Aguayo, Sergio. 1998a. "Electoral Observation and Democracy in Mexico," pp. 167–86. In *Electoral Observation and Democratic Transitions in Latin America*, edited by K.J. Middlebrook. San Diego: Center for U.S.-Mexican Studies at the University of California.

Aguayo, Sergio. 1998b. "Temas del futuro: Votando en el extranjero." *Reforma* (September 16, 1998).

Aguayo, Sergio. 1999. "Escandalo y reforma." *Reforma* (May 12, 1999).

Aguero, Felipe. 1995. *Soldiers, Civilians and Democracy: Post-Franco Spain in Comparative Perspective*. Baltimore: Johns Hopkins University Press.

Aguirre Beltrán, G. 1991. *Obra antropológica IV, Formas de gobierno indígena*. Mexico: Fondo de Cultura Económica.

Alba, Victor. 1969. *The Latin Americans*. New York: Praeger.

Alducin Abitia, Enrique. 1986. *Los valores de los mexicanos. Mexico: entre la tradiciones y la modernidad.* Mexico City: Fondo Cultural Banamex.

Alexander, Jeffrey C. 1983. *The Classical Attempt at Theoretical Synthesis: Max Weber.* Berkeley: University of California Press.

Alexander, Jeffrey C. 1991. "Bringing Democracy Back In: Universalistic Solidarity and the Civil Sphere," pp. 157–73. In *Intellectuals and Politics: Social Theory in a Changing World,* edited by C.C. Lemert. Newbury Park, CA: Sage Publications.

Alexander, Jeffrey C. and Philip Smith. 1993. "The Discourse of American Civil Society: A New Proposal for Cultural Studies." *Theory and Society,* 22: 51–207.

Alexander, Jeffrey C. et al. 1987. *The Micro-Macro Link,* edited by Jeffrey Alexander, Bernhard Giesen, Richard Munch, and Neil J. Smelser. Berkeley: University of California Press.

Alianza Cívica. 1994. "Observación 1994." Mexico City: Mexico.

Alianza Cívica. 1996. "Las Violaciones al derecho a la información de los mexicanos, [Violations of the Right of Mexicans to Information]." Mexico City: Mexico.

"Although the Supreme Court Cannot Involve Itself in Electoral Issues, Paradoxically, It Can Involve Itself in Electoral Questions: Castro y Castro." 1996. *Proceso* (November 6).

Amparo Cesar, Maria and de la Madrid, David. 1998. 'The 1997 Elections in Review." *Siempre,* 13: 13–24.

Anderson, L. 1991. "Political Pacts, Liberalism and Democracy: The Tunisian National Pact of 1988." *Government and Opposition,* 26(2): 244–60 (Spring).

Arato, Andrew. 1994. "Dilemmas Arising from the Power to Create Constitutions in Eastern Europe," pp. 165–65. In *Constitutionalism, Identity, Difference and Legitimacy,* edited by Michael Rosenfeld. Durham: Duke University Press.

Arco. 1995. *Constitucion Politica de los estados unidos mexicanos.* Mexico: Editorial Alco.

Ash, Timothy Garton. 1983. *The Polish Revolution: Solidarity.* New York: Charles Scribner & Sons.

Aubert, Vilhelm. 1983. *In Search of Law: Sociological Approaches to Law.* Oxford: Martin Robertson.

Bailey, John and Arturo Valenzeula. 1997. "The Shape of the Future." *Journal of Democracy,* 8(4), October, pp. 43–57.

Ballesteros, Corona and P. Cunningham. 1998. "The Rainbow at Midnight: Zapatistas and Autonomy." *Capital and Class,* 66: 12–22 (Autumn).

Baloyra, Enrique, ed. 1987. *Comparing New Democracies: Transition and Consolidation in Mediterranean Europe and the Southern Cone.* Boulder, CO: Westview Press.

Barkan, Joel D. 1994. "Divergence and Convergence in Kenya and Tanzania: Pressures for Reform," pp. 1–49. In *Beyond Capitalism versus Socialism in Kenya and Tanzania,* edited by Joel D. Barkan. London: Lynne Rienner.

Barragán, Javier Moctezuma. 1994. *Jose Maria Iglesias y la Justicia Electoral.* Mexico City: UNAM.

Bartra, Roger. 1989. "Changes in Political Culture: The Crisis of Nationalism," pp. 55–86. In *Mexico's Alternate Political Futures,* edited by Wayne A. Cornelius, Judith Gentleman, and Peter H. Smith. San Diego: Center for U.S.-Mexican Studies, University of California, Monograph Series, 30.

Beceríl, A. 1999. "New Call to Dialogue: COCOPA to the EZLN" [Nuevo llamado de la Cocopa al EZLN para dialogar], *La Jornada* (March 25).

Becerra, Pablo. 1997. "The Electoral System and Mexican Parties, the Interminable Transition, Notes on the 1996 Electoral Reform." *El Cotidiano*, 77–83 (January–February).

Beirne, Piers. 1979. "Ideology and Rationality in Max Weber's Sociology of Law," pp. 103–31. In *Research in Law and Sociology*, vol. 2. Greenwich, CT: JAI Press.

Bendix, Reinhard. 1962. "Legal Domination: The Emergence of Legal Rationality." In *Max Weber: An Intellectual Portrait.* New York: Doubleday.

Bollen, Kenneth. 1979. "Political Development and the Timing of Development." *American Sociological Review*, 44: 572–87.

Bollen, Kenneth. 1980. "Issues in the Comparative Measurement of Political Democracy," *American Sociological Review*, 45: 370–90.

Booth, John A. and Mitchell A. Seligson. 1993. "Paths to Democracy and the Political Culture of Costa Rica, Mexico and Nicaragua," pp. 107–62. In *Political Culture and Democracy in Developing Countries*, edited by Larry Diamond Boulder, CO: Lynne Rienner.

Botz, Dan La. 1995. *Democracy in Mexico: Peasant Rebellion and Political Reform.* Boston: South End Press.

Bratton, Michael. 1998. "Second Elections in Africa." *Journal of Democracy*, 9(3): 51–66.

Bratton, Michael and Nicolas van de Walle. 1994. "NeoPatrimonial Regimes and Political Transitions in Africa." *World Politics*, 46 (July): 453–89.

Bratton, Michael and Nicolas van de Walle. 1997. *Democratic Experiments in Africa: Regime Transitions in Comparative Perspective.* Cambridge: Cambridge University Press.

Brubaker, Rogers. 1984. "The Limits of Rationality" In *Controversies in Sociology*, edited by T.B. Bottomore and M.J. Mulkay. London: Routledge Press.

Brubaker, Rogers. 1998. "Immigration, Citizenship, and the Nation-State in France and Germany," pp. 131–64. In *The Citizenship Debates*, edited by Gershon Sharfir. Minneapolis: University of Minnesota Press.

Buendía, Jorge. 1996. "Economic Reform, Public Opinion, and Presidential Approval in Mexico, 1988–1993," *Comparative Political Studies*, 29(5) October, pp. 566–91.

Burgoa, Ignacio. 1951. *El Juicio de Amparo.* Mexico City: Porrua.

Buscaglia, Edgardo, Jr., Maria Dakolias, and William Ratliff. 1995. *Judicial Reform in Latin America: A Framework for National Development.* Stanford, CA: Hoover Institution.

Cain, Maureen. 1981. "The Limits of Idealism—Max Weber and the Sociology of Law." In *Research in Law and Sociology*, vol. 3, edited by S. Spitzer. Greenwich, CT: JAI Press.

Camin, H.A. 1997. "Autonomias Indigenas: Riesgos y Realidades." *Nexos* (January–February).

Camp, Roderic. 1993. *Politics in Mexico.* Oxford: Oxford University Press.

Carpizo, J. 1978. *El Presidencialismo en Mexico.* Mexico City: Siglo Veintiuno.

Carr, Raymond and Juan Pablo Fusi. 1981. *Spain: Dictatorship to Democracy.* 2nd ed. London: Unwin Hayman.

Centeno, Miguel Angel. 1994. *Democracy within Reason: Technocratic Revolution in Mexico.* University Park: Pennsylvania State University Press.

Centeno, Miguel Angel. 1997. "After the Fall: The Legacy of Carlos Salinas." *Mexican Studies*, 13(1): 201–14

Cepeda Neri, Andres. 1999. "Indigenous Rights and the *San Andrés* Accords." *La Jornada* (May 17).

Chazan, Naomi. 1994. "Engaging the State: Associational Life in Sub-Saharan Africa." In *State Power and Social Forces: Domination and Transformation.* Cambridge: Cambridge University Press.

Chege, M. 1994. "The Return of MultiParty Politics," pp. 47–74. In *Beyond Capitalism versus Socialism in Kenya and Tanzania,* edited by Joel D. Barkan. Boulder, CO: Lynne Rienner.

Cheng, T.J. 1989. "Democratizing the Quasi-Leninist Regime in Taiwan." *World Politics,* XLI(4) (July): 471–99.

Chia-Ling. 1998. "Paths to Democracy: Taiwan in Comparative Perspective." Ph.D. dissertation, Yale University.

Chipres, S.G. 1997. "Clergy Should Not Act Politically: Rivera" [Nadie en el clero debe hacer politica: Rivera]. *La Jornada* (June 16).

Chu, Yun-han. 1996. "Taiwan's Unique Challenges." *Journal of Democracy,* 7: 3.

CIDE (Centro de Docencia y Investigación Económica), 1991–94. Exit Polls, Mexico, Nuevo Leon, Coahuila, Morelos, Mexico City, Michoacan, Tabasco, Veracruz conducted by independent state polling institutes.

CIDE. 1991. Political Culture Surveys #1 and #2, Mexico City.

CIDE. 1997. Exit polls San Luis Potosú, Querétaro, Colima, Campeche Nuevo León conducted by *Reforma* investigative unit.

"Civic Alliance Cannot Have Electoral Monitors: Electoral Tribunal." 1997. *La Jornada* (February 15).

"Civic Alliance Queries Legitimacy of Elections." 1994. *La Jornada* (November 9).

Clagett, Helen. 1965. *The Administration of Justice in Latin America.* New York: Oceana.

Cliffe, Lionel. 1967. *One-Party Democracy: The 1965 Tanzanian General Elections.* Nairobi: East Africa Publishers.

Coatsworth, John H. 1983. "Orígenes del autoritarismo moderno en México." In *Orígenes del autoritarismo en American Latina,* edited by L. Allub. Mexico, D.F.: Editorial Katún.

Cohen, J. 1970. "Max Weber and the Dynamics of Rationalized Domination." *Telos,* 64–85.

Collier, David. 1979. "The Bureaucratic-Authoritarian Model: Synthesis and Priorities for Future Research." In *The New Authoritarianism in Latin America,* edited by D. Collier. Princeton: Princeton University Press.

Collier, Ruth. 1982. *Regimes in Tropical Africa.* Berkeley: University of California Press.

Collier, David and Ruth Collier. 1979. "Inducements versus Constraints: Disaggregating Corporatism." *American Political Science Review,* 73(4) (December): 967–86.

Collins, Randall. 1988. "Rationalization: The Master Trend of History?" In *Max Weber: A Skeleton Key,* Masters of Social Theory, 3, Beverly Hills, CA: Sage Publications.

Collins, Randall. 1998. "Democratization in World-Historical Perspective," pp. 14–31. In *Max Weber, Democracy and Modernization.* New York: St. Martin's Press.

Colclough, C. and S McCarthy. 1980. *The Political Economy of Botswana: A Study of Growth and Distribution.* Oxford: Oxford University Press.

Cornelius, Wayne A. 1986. "Political Liberalization and the 1985 Elections in Mexico." In *Elections and Democratization in Latin America, 1980–85,* edited by P.W. Drake and E. Silva. San Diego: Center for Iberian and Latin American Studies, University of California.

Cornelius, Wayne A., J. Gentleman, and P.H. Smith. 1989. "The Dynamics of Political Change in Mexico," pp. 1–54. In *Mexico's Alternative Political Futures,* edited by Wayne A. Cornelius, J. Gentleman, and P.H. Smith. San Diego: Center for U.S.-Mexican Studies, Monograph Series 30.

Costello, Matthew J. 1996. "Administration Triumphs over Politics: The Transformation of the Tanzanian State." *African Studies Review*, 39(1) (April): 123–48.

Cotler, Julio. 1979. "State and Regime: Comparative Notes on the Southern Cone and the 'Enclave' Societies," pp. 255–82. In *The New Authoritarianism in Latin America*, edited by D. Collier. Princeton: Princeton University Press.

Crenshaw, Edward. 1995. "Democracy and Demographic Inheritance: The Influence of Modernity and Proto-Modernity on Political and Civil Rights, 1965–1980." *American Sociological Review*, 60 (October): 702–18.

Crespo, Antonio. 1996. *Votar en los estados: analisis comparado de las legislaciones electorales estatales en Mexico*. Mexico City: Porrua.

Crouch, Harold. 1996. *Government and Society in Malaysia*. Ithaca: Cornell University Press.

Cruz, Consuelo and Rut C Diamint, Rut C. 1998. "The New Military Autonomy in Latin America." *Journal of Democracy*, 9(4): 115–22.

Dahl, Robert. 1989. *Democracy and Its Critics*. New Haven: Yale University Press.

"Debate over Mexican Migrants' Right to Vote Goes to the Heart of Questions about Democracy and Accountability." 1999. *Pacific News Service* (January 19).

De la Peza, J. 1997. "The Criticisms of the Electoral Tribunal Are Due to Incomprehension of its Role, Ignorance of the Law and the Novelty of the [Legal] Process: José Luis de la Peza." *Proceso*, 1–6 (June 15).

DePalma, Anthony. 1995. "Mexico Lives by Virtual Law." *New York Times* (March 26), E3.

Diario Oficial de la Federacion, December 31, 1994.

Diamond, Larry. 1992. "Economic Development and Democracy Considered," pp. 93–139. In *Reexamining Democracy: Essays in Honor of Seymour Martin Lipset*, edited by G. Marks and L. Diamond. Newbury Park, CA: Sage Publications.

Diamond, Larry. 1994. "Rethinking Civil Society: Toward Democratic Consolidation." *Journal of Democracy* 5 (July).

Diamond, Larry. 1996. "Causes and Effects," pp. 411–36. In *Political Culture and Democracy in Developing Countries*, edited by Larry Diamond. Boulder, CO: Lynne Rienner.

Diamond, Larry et al. 1989. *Democracy in Developing Countries*, edited by Larry Diamond, Juan Linz, and Seymour Martin Lipset. Boulder, CO: Lynne Rienner.

Díaz-Polanco, H. 1991. *Autonomia Regional: la autodeterminación de los pueblos indios*. Mexico City: Siglo Veintiuno.

Dicey, A.V. [1914] 1982. *The Law of the Constitution*. 8th ed. Indianapolis: Liberty Classics.

Dillon, S. 1998. "Mexico Considers Extending Presidential Vote to Immigrants in U.S." *New York Times* (December 7).

Dillon, S. 1999. "Zedillo Suggests U.S-Style System to Pick Nominees." *New York Times* (March 5), A1.

DiPalma, Giuseppe. 1990. *To Craft Democracies: An Essay on Democratic Transitions*. Berkeley: University of California Press.

Dix, Robert H. 1989. "Cleavage Structures and Party Systems in Latin America." *Comparative Politics*, 22(1):23–37.

Dominguez, Jorge I. and James McCann. 1995. "Shaping Mexico's Electoral Arena: The Construction of Partisan Cleavages in the 1988 and 1991 National Elections." APSR, 89(1) (March): 34–47.

Dragnich, Alex N. 1971. "The Judicial Process." In *Government and Politics*, 2d ed., edited by J.C. Wahlke and A. Dragnich. New York: Random House.

Dresser, Denise. 1998. "Mexico after the July 6 Election: Neither Heaven nor Hell." *Current History*, (February): 55–60.

Dresser, Denise. 1999. Presentation, Mexico's Elections 2000: Dilemmas of Democratization. UCLA Mellon Program in Latin American Sociology and the UCLA Latin American Center, May 5.

Dulce, Maria Jose Firinas. 1989. *La Sociologia del derecho de Max Weber*. Mexico City: UNAM.

The Economist, April 1, 1995: 36–37.

Edles, Desfor Laura. 1995. "Rethinking Democratic Transition: a Culturalist Critique and the Spanish Case." Theory and Society, 25: 355–84.

Eliason, Sven. 1998. "Max Weber and Plebiscitary Democracy," pp. 47–60. In *Max Weber, Democracy and Modernization*. New York: St. Martin's Press.

El Mundo. 1999. (November 21, 1999).

Emigh, Rebecca. 1996. "The Power of Negative Thinking: The Use of Negative Case Methodology in the Development of Sociological Theory." *Theory and Society*, 20.

Ewing, Sally. 1987. "Formal Justice and the Spirit of Capitalism: Max Weber's Sociology of Law." *Law & Society Review*, 21(3): 487–512.

"Expatriate Mexicans' Electoral Role Will Cut Two Ways." 1998. *Hispanic Link News Service* (December 20).

Excelsior. 1998a. "Democratic Deepening." (November 23).

Excelsior. 1998b. "Academics, the PRD and PAN Demand the Incorporation of the Vote of Mexican Residents in the US." (November 30).

Excelsior. 1999a. January 13.

Excelsior. 1999b. "The Legislative Powers Has Become a Main Protagonist in the Current Political Transformation." (March 15).

Excelsior. 1999c. "The Initiative on Indigenous Rights Complies with the San Andreas Accords." (March 31).

Excelsior. 1999d. "Constitutional Rupture." (November 8).

EZLN *Reformas*. 1996. "Constitutional Reforms Regarding Indigenous Rights: Comparative Chart of the COCOPA and the EZLN-Federal Government Accords Signed on February 16, 1996." Internet Edition: http: //www.ezln.org/

EZLN Transición a la Democracia. 1996. "Special Forum for the Reform of the State, Theme 3: Transition to Democracy, June 30, 1996–July 6, 1996." Internet Edition: http: //www.ezln.org/ezln960914.htm/

Factor, Regis and Turner, Stephan. 1994. *Max Weber: The Lawyer as Social Thinker*. London: Routledge.

Factor Tiempo. 1999. "Time Factor: The Principal Obstacle to the Vote for Mexican Residents in the US." [Factor Tiempo, el Obstaculo Principal Para que Voten los Residentes Mexicanos]. *Excelsior* (March 10).

Faesler, J. 1999. "Our Vote Abroad." [Nuestro Vote en el exterior]. *Reforma* (March 23).

Feldman, Stephen M. 1991. "An Interpretation of Max Weber's Theory of Law: Metaphysics, Economics, and the Iron Cage of Constitutional Law." *Law & Social Inquiry*, 20.

Fine, Bob. 1984. *Democracy and the Rule of Law: Liberal Ideas and Marxist Critiques*. London: Pluto Press.

Finer, Herman. 1956. *Governments of Greater European Powers*. New York: Henry Holt & Co.

Fix-Fierro, Hector. 1995. "La Reforma Judicial y Las Acciones de Inconstitucionalidad," *Ius Revista*, Alonso Lujambio Irazabal, "Las reformas al Poder Judicial, una aproximacion desde la ciencia politica, *Reformas*.

Fix-Zamudio, Hector & Cossio Diaz, Jose Ramon. 1995. *El Poder Judicial en el ordamiento mexicano*. Mexico City: Fondo de Cultura Economica.

Fox, Jonathan and Luis Hernandez. 1995. "Lessons from the Mexican Election." *Dissent*, 29–33 (Winter).

Freund, Julien. 1968. "The Sociology of Law." In *The Sociology of Max Weber*. New York: Pantheon Books.

Fredrich, C.J. and K. Brezenski Zbigniew. 1956. *Totalitarian Dictatorship and Autocracy*. Cambridge: Harvard University Press.

Garcia, Carlos Arellano. 1981. *El Juicio de Amparo*. Mexico, D.F.: Siglo Veintiuno.

Garreton, Manual Antonio. 1992. "The Political Evolution of the Chilean Military Regime and Problems in the Transition to Democracy," pp. 95–122. In *Elites and Democratic Consolidation in Latin America and Southern Europe*, edited by Richard Gunther and J. Higley. Cambridge: Cambridge University Press.

Garrido, J.L. 1982. *El Partido de la Revolución Institucionalizada: La Formación del nuevo estado en mexico (1928–1945)*. Mexico City: Siglo Veintiuno.

Garrido, J.L. 1989. "The Crises of Presidentialism," pp. 417–34. In *Mexico's Alternative Political Futures*, edited by Wayne A. Cornelius, J. Gentleman, and P.H. Smith. Sand Diego: Center for U.S.-Mexican Studies, University of California, Monograph Series, 30.

Garrido, J.L. 1999. The Referendum [La Consulta], *La Jornada* (March 20).

GEA Político. 1996. 10 December 1996 Bulletin, pp. 11–15.

Geddes, Barbara. 1994. "Challenging the Conventional Wisdom." *Journal of Democracy*, 5(4) (October): 104–18.

Geddes, Barbara. 1995. "Games of Intra-Regime Conflict and the Breakdown of Authoritarianism." Paper presented at American Political Science Association, September 1995.

Geddes, Barbara. 1999. "What Do We Know about Democratization after Twenty Years?" *Annual Review of Political Science,* vol. 2, forthcoming.

Gellner, Ernest. 1994. *Conditions of Liberty: Civil Society and Its Rivals*. New York: Penguin Press.

Gibson, Edward L. 1997. "The Populist Road to Market Reform: Policy and Electoral Coalitions in Mexico and Argentina." *World Politics*, 49 (April): 339–70.

Gillespie, Charles Guy. 1992. "The Role of Civil-military Pacts in Elite Settlements and Elite Convergence: Democratic Consolidation in Uruguay," pp. 178–207. In *Elites and Democratic Consolidation in Latin American and Southern Europe*, edited by John Higley and Richard Gunther. Cambridge: Cambridge University Press.

Gillman, Howard. 1994. "On Constructing a Science of Comparative Judicial Politics: Tate & Haynie's 'Authoritarianism and the Functions of Courts,' " *Law & Society Review,* 28(2): 355–76.

Gilly, Adolfo. 1994. *El cardenismo, una utopía mexicana*. Mexico City: Cal y arena.

Giménez, Rafeal. Federal District Exit Poll, Research Unit of *Reforma*, July 6, 1997.

Gomez, E.T. 1996. "Electoral Funding of General, State and Party Elections in Malaysia," *Journal of Contemporary Asia,* 26(1): 81–99.

Gomez-Tagle, Silva. 1994. *De la alquimia al fraude en los elecciones mexicanas*. Mexico: GV Editores.

Gonzalez Casanova, Pablo. 1965. *La Democracia en Mexico*, Mexico City: Ediciones ERA.

Gordillo, E.E. 1998. " PRI: Opportunities and Risks in Consulting the Party Bases." [PRI: consulta a las bases, oportunidades y riesgos]. *La Jornada* (June 1).

Green, J. 1998. "The Slow Breakup of the PRI's corporate unionism in Mexico." *Communist Voice* (January 20).

Gunther, Richard, Nikiforos P. Diamandouros, and Puhle Hans-Jurgen. 1995. *The Politics of Democratic Consolidation: Southern Europe in Comparative Perspective.* Baltimore: Johns Hopkins University Press.

Gunther, Richard, Nikiforos P. Diamandouros, and Puhle Hans-Jurgen. 1996. "O'Donnell's 'Illusions': A Rejoinder." *Journal of Democracy*, 7(4): 151–59.

Gunther, Richard and J. Higley, eds. 1992. *Elites and Democratic Consolidation in Latin America and Southern Europe.* Cambridge: Cambridge University Press.

Habermas, Jurgen. 1971. "Technology and Science as 'Ideology,' " pp. 81–122. In *Toward a Rational Society.* London: Heinemann.

Hall, John A., ed. 1995. *Civil Society: Theory, History and Comparisons.* London: Polity Press.

Halsey, A.H. 1984. "T.H. Marshall: Past and Present, 1893–1981." *Sociology*, 18.

Hamilton, Nora. 1982. *The Limits of State Autonomy: Post-Revolutionary Mexico.* Princeton: Princeton University Press.

Harvard Law Review. 1995. "Liberalismo contra Democracia: Recent Judicial Reform in Mexico." *Harvard Law Review,* 108(8) (June): 1919–36.

Harvey, N. 1994. *Rebellion in Chiapas.* Transformation of Rural Mexico Series, no. 5. La Jolla: Center for U.S.-Mexican Studies, University of California San Diego.

Hellman, Judith Adler. 1997. "Continuity and Change in the Mexican Political System." *European Review of Latin American and Caribbean Studies*, 63 (December): 91–99.

Holm, John D. 1988. "Botswana: A Paternalistic Democracy?" pp. 179–216. In *Democracy in Developing Countries.* Boulder, CO: Lynne Reinner.

Huerta, I. 1993. "Notes sobre la historia de un régime particular: Mexico." Manuscript, Universidad Complutense, Madrid: España.

Huff, Tony E. 1989. "On Weber, Law and Universalism: Some Preliminary Considerations." *The Comparative Civilizations Review*, 21 (Fall): 47–79.

Hunt, Alan. 1978. *The Sociological Movement in Law.* London: Macmillan Press.

Huntington, Samuel. 1970. "Social and Institutional Dynamics of One-Party Systems," pp. 3–45. In *Authoritarian Politics in Modern Society*, edited by Samuel P. Huntington and Clement H. Moore. New York: Basic Books.

Huntington, S. 1991. *The Third Wave: Democratization in the Late Twentieth Century.* Norman: University of Oklahoma Press.

Huntington, Samuel. 1994. "Will More Countries Become Democratic?" *Political Science Quarterly*, 99: 193–218.

"IFE: Only Nine Citizens Can Participate in the Elections." 1997. *La Jornada* (January 16).

"IFE Urges Congress to Legislate Voting System." 1998. *Associated Press* (September 3).

IFES Report 1995. Cited in Killian 1998.

"Immigrants in U.S. Going 'Transnational.' " 1996. *New York Times News Service* (December 30).

INEGI 1990. Instituto Nacional Estadistica Geografica e Informatica, Aguascalientes, Mexico.

INEGI 1995. Instituto Nacional Estadistica Geografica e Informatica, Aguascalientes, Mexico.

Informe Presidential. 1998. Office of the Mexican Presidency.

Inkeles, Alex, ed. 1991. *On Measuring Democracy: Its Consequences and Concomitants.* New York: Transaction Publishers.

Institute for Juridic Studies. 1995. Personal interview, UNAM, Mexico City, August 28, 1995.

Janos, Andrew C. 1970. "The One-Party State and Social Mobilization: East Europe between the Wars," pp. 239–60. In *Authoritarian Politics in Modern Society: The Dynamics of Established One-Party Systems*, edited by S.P. Huntington and C.H. Moore. New York: Basic Books.

Jowitt, Kenneth. 1974. An Organizational Approach to the Study of Political Culture in Marxist-leninist Systems. *American Political Science Review*, 69: 1171–91.

Jurisprudencia. 1985. Poder Judicial de la Federacion. Tesis Ejecutorias, 1917–1985. Apendice al Semanario Juridicial de la Federacion. Octava Parte. Jurisprudencia Comun al Pleno y las Salas. Mexico, p. 272.

Kalberg, S. 1980. "Max Weber's Types of Rationality: Cornerstones for the Analysis of Rationalization Process in History." *American Journal of Sociology*, 85: 1145–79.

Karl, Terry Lynn. 1986. "Petroleum and Political Pacts: The Transition to Democracy in Venezuela." In *Transitions from Authoritarian Rule: Prospects for Democracy*, edited by Guillermo O'Donnell, Philippe C. Schmitter, Laurence Whitehead. Baltimore: Johns Hopkins University Press.

Katz, Jonathan N. and Gary King. 1999. "A Statistical Model for Multiparty Electoral Data." *American Political Science Review*, 93(1) (March): 15–32.

Kaufman, Robert R. and Leo Zuckerman. 1998. "Attitudes Toward Economic Reform in Mexico: The Role of Political Orientations." *American Political Science Review*, 92(2): 359–75.

Kendall, P.L. and K.M. Wolfe. 1949. "The Analysis of Deviant Cases in Communications Research." In *Communications Research, 1948–1949*, edited by Paul F. Lazarfeld and Frank N. Stanton. New York: Harper & Brothers.

Kiewiet, D. Roderick and Donald R. Kinder. 1981. "Sociotropic Politics: The American Case." *British Journal of Political Science*, 11: 129–61.

Killian, Bernadeta. 1998. "Sources of Popular Support for Democratic Change in Tanzania." Working Paper, Political Science Department, University of Tanzania, Dar Es Salaam, Tanzania.

King, Ambrose Y.C. 1993. "A Nonparadigmatic Search for Democracy in a Post-Confucian Culture: The Case of Taiwan, R.O.C," pp. 139–62. In *Political Culture and Democracy in Developing Countries*, edited by Larry Diamond. Boulder, CO: Lynne Rienner.

Klesner, Joseph L. 1995. "The 1994 Mexican Elections: Manifestation of a Divided Society?" *Mexican Studies*, 11(1) (Winter): 138–49.

Knight, Alan. 1992. "Mexico's Elite Settlement: Conjuncture and Consequences," pp. 113–45. In *Elites and Democratic Consolidation in Latin America and Southern Europe.* Cambridge: Cambridge University Press.

Krieger, Emilio. 1994. *En Defensa de la Constitucion: Violaciones Presidenciales a la Carta Magna.* Mexico, D.F.: Grijalbo.

Kronman, Anthony T. 1983. *Max Weber.* Stanford: Stanford University Press.

Kymlicka, W. 1998. "Multicultural Citizenship," pp. 167–88. In *The Citizenship Debates*, edited by Gershon Sharfir. Minneapolis: University of Minnesota Press.

La Jornada. (May 31, 1996); (November 1, 1995); (June 26, 1995); (August 4, 1995); (October 3, 1995); (July 3, 1996); (July 8, 1996); (August 16, 1996); (January 8, 1997a); (June 2, 1997b).

La Jornada. 1998a. "Vote Abroad." [Voto en el extranjero]. *La Jornada* (November 21).

La Jornada. 1998b. "Los salarios, en el menor nivel de 38 anos, revelan cifras oficiales." (November 22).

La Jornada. 1999. "Descarta Palacios una atomizacion sindical entre empleados del Estado." (May 16).

Las elecciones primarias. 1998. "The PRI primary elections." [Las elecciones primarias priistas]. *La Jornada* (June 4).

Latin American Data Base. 1996. February 26, Vol. 2, No. 18. University of New Mexico.

Lawson, Chappell. 1998. "Why Cárdenas Won: The 1997 Elections in Mexico City," pp. 147–73. In *Toward Mexico's Democratization: Parties, Campaigns, Elections and Public Opinion,* edited by Jorge I. Domínguez and Alejandro Poiré. New York: Routledge.

Lear McConnell, Sharon. 1996. "Alianza Civica: Un nuevo actor no gubernmental en el ambito politico mexicano." Ph.D. dissertation, Facultad Latinoamericano de Ciencias Sociales, Mexico City, Mexico.

Levine, Donald N. 1985. *The Flight from Ambiguity: Essays on Social and Cultural Theory.* Chicago: University of Chicago Press.

Levy, Daniel C. 1989. "Mexico: Sustained Civilian Rule without Democracy." In *Democracy in Developing Countries: Latin American,* edited by L. Diamond, J.J. Linz, and S.M. Lipset. Boulder, CO: Lynne Rienner.

Linz, Juan J. 1975. "Totalitarian and Authoritarian Regimes," pp. 175–412. In *The Handbook of Political Science, vol. 3: Macropolitical Theory,* edited by F.I. Greenstein and N.W. Polsby. Reading, MA: Addison-Welsley.

Linz, Juan J. 1978a. "From Great Hopes to Civil War: the Breakdown of Democracy in Spain." In *The Breakdown of Democratic Regimes: Europe,* edited by Juan A. Linz and A. Stepan. Baltimore: Johns Hopkins University Press.

Linz, Juan J. 1978b. "Non-Competitive Elections in Europe," pp. 36–65. In *Elections without Choice.* London: Macmillan Press.

Linz, Juan J. 1990. "Transitions to Democracy." *Washington Quarterly* 13.

Linz, Juan J. and Alfred Stephan. 1996. *Problems in Democratic Transition and Consolidation: Southern Europe, South America, and Postcommunist Europe.* Baltimore: Johns Hopkins University Press.

Lipjart, Arend and Carlos H. Waisman. 1996. *Institutional Design in New Democracies: Eastern Europe and Latin America.* Boulder, CO: Westview Press.

Lipset, Seymour Martin. 1959. "Some Social Requisites of Democracy: Economic Development and Political Legitimacy," *American Political Science Review* 53 (1959): 71–85.

Lipset, Seymour Martin. 1973. "Tom Marshall—Man of Wisdom." *British Journal of Sociology,* 24.

Lipset, Seymour Martin [1960] 1981. *Political Man: The Social Bases of Politics.* Expanded ed. Baltimore Johns Hopkins University Press.

Lipset, Seymour Martin. 1994. "The Social Requisites of Democracy Revisited." *American Sociological Review,* 59(1) (February): 1–22.

Lipset, S., & Rokkan, Stein. [1967] 1985. "Cleavage Structures, Party Systems, and Voter Alignments," pp. 113–85. In *Consensus and Conflict: Essays in Political Sociology.* New Brunswick, NJ: Transaction Publishers.

Lipset, Seymour Martin, Seong Kyoung-Ryung, and Torres, John Charles. 1993. "A Comparative Analysis of the Social Requisites of Democracy." *International Social Science*, 45: 155–75.

Lipset, Seymour Martin, M. Trow, and J. Coleman. 1956. *Union Democracy: The Inside Politics of the International Typographical Union.* New York: Free Press.

Lockwood, D. 1974. "For TH. Marshall." *Sociology*, 8.

Loewith, Karl. 1970. "Weber's Interpretation of the Bourgeois-Capitalist World in Terms of the Guiding Principle of 'Rationalization.' " In *Max Weber*, edited by D. Wrong. Englewood Cliffs, NJ: Prentice-Hall.

Loeza, Soledad. 1985. "El llamado de las urnas, para que sirven las eleccciones in Mexico?" pp. 75–83. In *Poder Local, Poder Regional.* Mexico City: Mexico.

Loeza, Soledad. 1989. "The Emergence and Legitimization of the Modern Right, 1970–1988," pp. 351–60. In *Mexico's Alternative Political Futures*, edited by Wayne A. Corneilius, J. Gentleman, and P.H. Smith. San Diego: Center for U.S.-Mexican Studies, Monograph Series 30.

Loeza, Soledad. 1997. "Partido Accion Nacional: Opposition and the Government in Mexico," pp. 23–35. In *Mexico: Assessing Neo-Liberal Reform.* London: Institute of Latin American Studies.

Lopez, J.H. 1998. Report, *La Jornada* (June 20).

Luebbert, Gregory M. 1991. *Liberalism, Fascism or Social Democracy.* New York: Oxford University Press.

Mabry, Donald J. 1973. *Mexico's Accion Nacional: A Catholic Alternative to Revolution.* Syracuse: Syracuse University Press.

MacLeod, Dag. 1999. "Political Realignment in Mexico: The PRD Moves from 'Show' to 'Place.' " Working Paper #20, Program in Comparative and International Development, Johns Hopkins University.

Madrazo, Jorge. 1997. "Introduction," pp. 1–12. In *Tradiciones y Costumbres Juridicas*, edited by Estrada Martinez. Mexico City: CNDH.

Magaloni, Beatriz. 1998. "Is the PRI Fading? Economic Performance, Electoral Accountability, and Voting Behavior in the 1994 and 1997 Elections," pp. 203–36. In *Toward Mexico's Democratization: Parties, Campaigns, Elections and Public Opinion*, edited by Jorge I. Domínguez and Alejandro Poiré. New York: Routledge.

Mann, Michael. 1987. "Ruling Class Strategies and Citizenship." *Sociology*, 21(3) (August): 339–54.

Mann, Michael. 1993. *The Sources of Social Power, Vol. II: The Rise of Classes and Nation-States, 1760–1914.* Cambridge: Cambridge University Press.

Malo, Miguel Concha. 1994. "Los Derechos Políticos como Derechos Humanos. Concepción y Defensa," pp. 15–28. In *Los derechos políticos como derechos humanos*, edited by Miguel Concha Malo. Mexico City: UNAM.

Marcuse, Herbert. 1968. "Industrialization and Capitalism in the Work of Max Weber." In *Negations—Essays in Critical Theory.* London: Allen Lane.

Markoff, John. 1996. *Waves of Democracy.* Thousand Oaks, CA: Pine Forge Press.

Marsh, Norman. 1961. "The Rule of Law as a Supra-National Concept," pp. 224–62. In *Oxford Essays in Jurisprudence.* Oxford: Oxford University Press.

Marshall, T.H. 1963. *Class, Citizenship and Social Development.* Westport, CT: Greenwood Press.

Melgar Adalid, Mario. 1995. *Reformas al Poder Judicial* (Reforms of the Judicial Power), edited by Mario Melgar Adalid. Mexico City: UNAM.

Merkl, Peter H. 1993. "Which Are Today's Democracies?" *International Social Science Journal,* 45: 257–70.

Meyer, Lorenzo. 1989. "Democratization of the PRI: Mission Impossible?" pp. 325–50. In *Mexico's Alternative Political Futures,* edited by W.A. Cornelius, J. Gentleman, and P.H. Smith. San Diego: Center for U.S.-Mexican Studies, University of California, Monograph Series, 30.

Meyer, Lorenzo. 1998a. "Transicion, consolidacion y confusion." *Reforma* (October 22).

Meyer, Lorenzo. 1998b. *Fin de Régimen y Democracia Incipiente.* Mexico City: Editorial Oceano.

Meyer, Lorenzo. 1994. *Una Breve Historia de Mexico.* Mexico City: El Colegio de Mexico.

Meyer, Michael C. and William L. Sherman. 1983. *The Course of Mexican History.* 2nd ed. New York: Oxford University Press.

Middlebrook, Kevin J. 1986. "Political Liberalization in an Authoritarian Regime: The Case of Mexico." In *Transitions from Authoritarian Rule,* vol. 3, edited by G. O'Donnell, P. Phillippe Schmitter, and L. Whitehead. Baltimore: Johns Hopkins University Press.

Miranda, Creel, Santiago. 1999. "Mitos legislativos," *Reforma* (June 30).

Mizrahi, Yemile. 1995. "Democracia, eficiencia y participacion: los dilemas de los gobiernos de oposicion en Mexico." *Politica y Gobierno,* 2: 177–205.

Molutsi, P.P. and John D. Holm. 1989. "Introduction," pp. 1–9. In *Democracy in Botswana.* Athens: Ohio University Press.

Mommsen, W.J. 1983. "The Antinomian Structure of Max Weber's Political Thought." *Current Perspectives in Social Theory,* 4: 289–311.

Monasterio, Leonor Ortiz. 1996. "Letter from Office of the Mexican Presidency." Annex #3 in "Las Violaciones al Derecho a la Informacion de los Mexicanos: La Demanda de Amparo de Alianza Civica contra la presidencia de la republica." Mexico City: Mexico.

Montes, A.R. 1999. "The Indigenist Referendum and Discursive Spins." [La consulta indígena y los enredos discursivos], *La Jornada* (March 20).

Monsivais, Carlos. 1978. "1968–1978: Notas sobre cultura y sociedad en Mexico." *Cuadernos Politicos* 17.

Moore, Barrington. 1966. *The Social Origins of Dictatorship and Democracy.* Boston: Beacon Press.

Moore, Clement H. 1970. "The Single Party as Source of Legitimacy," pp. 48–74. In *Authoritarian Politics in Modern Society: The Dynamics of Established One-Party Systems,* edited by S.P. Huntington and C.H. Moore. New York: Basic Books.

Morgan, Edmund Morris and Fraces X. Dwyer. 1946. *Introduction to the Study of Law.* Chicago: Callaghan.

Murrillo, Victoria M. 1997. "A Strained Alliance: Continuity and Change in Mexican Labour Politics," pp. 53–74. In *Mexico: Assessing Neo-Liberal Reform.* London: Institute of Latin American Studies.

Nash, J. 1995. "The Reassertion of Indigenous Identity: Mayan Responses to State Intervention in Chiapas." *Latin American Research Review* 30(3): 7–42.

Nassif, Alberto Aziz. 1989. "Regional Dimensions of Democratization," pp. 87–108. In *Mexico's Alternative Political Futures*, edited by Wayne A. Corneilius, J. Gentleman, and P.H. Smith. San Diego: Center for U.S.-Mexican Studies, Monograph Series 30.

National Indigenous Institute. 1995. "Socioeconomic Indicators of the Indigenous Speaking Population in Localities with 70% and above." In *Indicadores Socioeconomicas de los Pueblos Indígenas de Mexico*. Mexico City: Office of the Mexican Presidency.

Neuhouser, Kevin. 1992. "Democratic Stability in Venezuela: Elite Consensus or Class Compromise?" *American Sociological Review*, 57(135) (February).

The News. 1999. "Congress to Seek Ruling on Access to Books of Bankrupt Banco Union." (July 28).

No Clergy. 1997. "Clergy should not act politically: Rivera" [Nadie en el clero debe hacer politica: Rivera]. *La Jornada* (June 16).

Nyerere, Julis K. 1974. *Ujamma ni imani*. Dar es Salaam: EAPH.

O'Donnell, Guillermo. 1979. "Reflections on the Patterns of Change in the Bureaucratic-Authoritarian State." *Latin American Research Review*, 13(2).

O'Donnell, Guillermo. 1996. "Illusions about Consolidation." *Journal of Democracy*, 7(2): 34–51.

O'Donnell, Guillermo and Phillippe Schmitter. 1986. *Transitions from Authoritarian Rule: Tentative Conclusions about Uncertain Democracies*. Baltimore: John Hopkins University Press.

Oropeza, Manuel Gonzalez. 1995. "Justice by Challenge: The Administration of Justice and the Rule of Law in Mexico." *Institute for Juridic Investigations*, UNAM Manuscript, Mexico City.

Padgett, Vincent. 1976. *The Mexican Political System*. Boston: Houghton Mifflin.

Pardinas, Juan E. and Amezcua, Adriana. 1997. *Todos los gobernadores del Presidente: cuando el dedo de uno aplasta el voto popular*. Mexico, D.F.: Grijalbo.

Parson, J. 1982. *Botswana: Liberal Democracy and the Labor Reserve in Southern Africa*. Boulder, CO: Westview Press.

Pastor, Robert A., ed. 1989. *Democracy in the Americas: Stopping the Pendulum*. New York: Holmes and Meier.

Patterson, Wendy. 1999. "Mexican-Americans Want Right to Vote." *Los Angeles Times* (June 2).

Pei, Minxin. 1994. "The Puzzle for East Asian Exceptionalism." *Journal of Democracy*, 5 (October): 90–103.

Peschard, Jacqueline. 1997. "Participacion: Forma es fondo." *Nexos*, 9 (August): 9–10.

Pia Lara, Maria. 1997. "The Frail Emergence of Mexico's Democracy: Conquering the Public Space." *Thesis II*, 1–29.

Pinchetti, José. 1999. "Transition to Democracy?" *Reforma* (May 21).

Poiré, Alejandro. 1998. "Retrospective Voting, Partisanship, and Loyalty in Presidential Elections: 1994," pp. 24–56. In *Toward Mexico's Democratization: Parties, Campaigns, Elections and Public Opinion*, edited by Jorge I. Domínguez and Alejandro Poiré. New York: Routledge.

Pravda, Alex 1978. "Elections in Communist Party States," pp. 169–95. In *Elections Without Choice*. London: Macmillian Press.

PRD [Partido de la Revolución Democratica]. 1996. "En Defensa de los Derechos Humanos: Un Sexenio de violencia política," Secretaria de derechos humanos, Grupo Parlamentario, Mexico City.

"Preferible una costosa transicion." [A Costly Political Transition is Preferable to Perpetuating Corruption Affirms Bours]. 1998. *La Jornada* (June 29).

Presidencia [Office of the Mexican Presidency]. 1998a. "Observations of the Federal Government to the COCOPA initiatives and the San Andres Larrainzar Accords regarding Indigenous Rights and Culture." February 2, 1998.

Presidencia [Office of the Mexican Presidency]. 1998b. "Initiative of Constitutional Reformas in Indigenous Rights and Culture presented by the Federal Executive to the Mexican Congress."

Presidencia [Office of the Mexican Presidency]. 1995. "Law for Dialogue, Reconciliation and a Dignified Peace in Chiapas, March 9, 1995."

Presidential Commission Report on Party System in Tanzania. 1992. Dar El Salaam, Tanzania.

Preston, J. 1999. "Mexican Rebels, Showing Flare for Politics, Hold a Referendum." *New York Times* (March 22), A5.

PRI: Consulta. 1999. "PRI: opportunities and risks in consulting the party bases." [PRI: consulta a las bases, oportunidades y riesgos]. *La Jornada* (June 1).

Proceso, 946, 1995: 32–39; 951, 1995: 39; 980, 1995: 32–36; 984, 1995: 10–11; 985, 1995: 16–20; 992, 1995: 32–36; 1016, 1996: 16–22; 1023, 1996: 7–8; 1049, 1996: 9; April 1999.

Przeworski, Adam. 1986. "Some Problems in the Study of the Transition to Democracy," pp. 47–64. In Transitions from Authoritarian Rule: Prospects for Democracy, edited by Guillermo O'Donnell, Philippe C. Schmitter, and Laurence Whitehead. Baltimore: Johns Hopkins University Press.

Przeworski, Adam and Limongi, Fernando. 1997. "Modernization: Theories and Facts." *World Politics*, 49: 155–83.

Ramirez, Felipe Tena. 1994. *Leyes Fundamentales en Mexico, 1808–1994*, 11th ed. Mexico City: Siglo Veintiuno.

Raz, Joseph. 1979. *The Authority of Law*. Oxford: Clarendon Press.

REDET Baseline Survey Report. 1997. Conducted by Political Science Department, University of Dar El Salaam, Tanzania.

Reforma. 1995. (August 21), 5A.

Reforma. 1997. "1997 Election Results." (July 7).

Reforma. 1998. (July 13).

Reforma. 1999."Nayarit." (June 17).

Remmer, Karen L. 1991. "New Wine or Old Bottlenecks: The Study of Latin American Democracy." *Comparative Politics*, (July): 479–95.

Remmer, Karen L. 1995. "New Theoretical Perspectives on Democratization."*Comparative Politics*, 27 (October).

"Results of the Federal District Citizen Councilor Elections." 1995. *La Jornada* (November 1).

Reyna, José Luis. 1977. "Redefining the Authoritarian Regime." In *Authoritarianism in Mexico*, edited by J.L. Reyna and R.S. Weinert. Philadelphia: Institute for the Study of Human Issues.

Rex, John. 1961. *Key Problems in Sociological Theory*. London: Routledge and Kegan Paul.

Rheinstein, Max. 1954. *Max Weber on Law in Economy and Society*, edited with introduction and annotations. Cambridge: Harvard University Press.

Rich, P. 1997. "Nafta and Chiapas." *The Annals of the American Academy of Political and Social Science,* 550 (March): 72–84.

Rifkin, J.M. 1998. "Want Dual Citizenship? You Can Have It!" *Hispanic Times Magazine*, 19(3) (May–June): 14–15.

Rivapalacio, R. 1998. *Reforma* (October 16).

Rivera, Olvera A.J. 1998. "The PRI Primary Elections." [Las elecciones primarias priistas]. *La Jornada* (June 4).

Roett, Riordan. 1995. *The Challenge of Institutional Reform in Mexico*. Boulder: CO: Lynne Rienner.

Rokkan, Stein. 1961. "Mass Suffrage, Secret Voting and Political Participation." *Archives of European Sociology*, 11: 132–52.

Rokkan, Stein. 1970. *Citizens, Elections, Parties: Approaches to the Comparative Study of the Processes of Development*. New York: McKay.

Ross Pineda, R. 1999. "Vote Abroad Stuck in Congress." [Voto extraterritorial atorado en el Congreso]. *La Jornada* (March 26).

Rueschmeyer, Dietrich, Evelyne Huber Stevens, and John D. Stevens. 1992. *Capitalist Development and Democracy*. Chicago: University of Chicago Press.

Samstead, J. and Ruth Collier. 1995. "Mexican Labor and Structural Reform under Salinas: New Unionism or Old Stalemate?" pp. 1–37. In *The Challenge of Institutional Reform in Mexico*, edited by Riorden Reott. Boulder, CO: Lynne Rienner.

San Francisco Chronicle. 1996. "Mexico's PRI Thwarts Reforms." (December 16), A11.

Santibáñez, J.J. and V. Gonzalo. 1997. "Municipalities and Traditions: The Juridic Customs of the Mazateco People" [Municipios y Tradiciones: la Costumbres Juridicas del Pueblo Mazateco], pp. 13–26. In *Tradiciones y Costumbres Juridicas*, edited by Estrada Martinez. Mexico City: CNDH.

Schatz, Sara. 1998. "A Neo-Weberian Approach to Constitutional Courts in the Transition from Authoritarian Rule: The Mexican Case (1994–1997)." *International Journal of the Sociology of Law*, 26: 217–44.

Schedler, Andreas. 1998. "Mexico's Veiled Transition to Democracy." Manuscript prepared for the American Political Science Association Annual Meeting, Boston.

Schluchter, Wolfgang. 1979. "The Paradox of Rationalization and Value-neutrality and the Ethic of Responsibility," pp. 11–16. In *Max Weber's Vision of History*, edited by Guenther Roth and Wolfgang Schluchter. Berkeley: University of California Press.

Schluchter, Wolfgang. 1981. *The Rise of Western Rationalism: Max Weber's Developmental History*. Berkeley: University of California Press.

Schmitter, P.C. and T.L. Karl. 1994. "The Conceptual Travels of Transitologists and Consolidologists: How Far to the East Should They Attempt to Go?" *Slavic Review*, 53(1) (Spring): 173–85.

Schwartzman, Kathleen. 1998. "Globalization and Democracy." *Annual Review of Sociology*, 24: 159–81.

Scott, Robert E. 1964. *Mexican Government in Transition*. Urbana: University of Illinois Press.

Scott, Robert C. 1965. "Mexico: The Established Revolution," pp. 330–71. In *Political Culture and Political Development*. Princeton: Princeton University Press.

Secretaria de Trabajo. 1996. "Worker-Business Sector Dialogue Toward a New Laboral Culture." [Dialogo Obrero-Empresarial Hacia Una Nueva Cultura Laboral]. Mexico City: Mexico.

Semanario Judicial de la Federacion y Su Gaceta. 1996. "9na Epoca, Tomo 111, March 1996." *Stanford Journal of International Law*, 1995 (31): 423.

"Senate Unanimously Passes Dual Nationality Initiative." 1996. *The News* (December 6).

Shin, Doh Chull. 1994. "On the Third Wave of Democratization: A Synthesis and Evaluation of Recent Theory and Research." *World Politics* 47 (October): 135–70.

Shin, Doh Chull and Huoyan Shyu. 1997. "Political Ambivalence in South Korea and Taiwan." *Journal of Democracy*, 8(3): 108–21.

Siempre. 1999. "The HardLine Sexenio." [El Sexenio Duro]. 2385 (March 4): 36–37.

Smelser, Neil J. 1976. *Comparative Methods in the Social Sciences.* Englewood Cliffs, NJ: Prentice-Hall.

Smelser, Neil J. 1999. *Social Paralysis and Social Change*. Berkeley: University of California Press.

Smith, Anthony. 1998. "Mexico's Dual Citizenship Debate." *Los Angeles Times* (May 29).

Snyder, Richard. 1992. "Explaining Transitions from Neopatrimonial Dictatorships." *Comparative Politics*, 24: 379–400.

Soriano, A. 1999. "Time Factor: The Principal Obstacle to the Vote for Mexican Residents in the US." [Factor Tiempo, el Obstaculo Principal Para que Voten los Residentes Mexicanos]. *Excelsior* (March 10).

Soysal, Yasemin. 1998. "Toward a Postnational Model of Membership," pp. 189–220. In *The Citizenship Debates*, edited by Gershon Shafir. Minneapolis: University of Minnesota Press.

Spalding, Ruth. 1981. "The Mexican Variant of Corporatism." *Comparative Political Studies* 14 (July): 139–61.

Staniszkis, Jadwiga. 1984. *Poland's Self-Limiting Revolution*, edited by Jan T. Gross. Princeton: Princeton University Press.

Stark, D. and L. Bruszt. 1997. *Postsocialist Pathways: Transforming Politics and Property in East Central Europe*. Cambridge: Cambridge University Press.

Stavenhagen, R. 1995. "Indigenous Peoples: Emerging Actors in Latin America," pp. 1–15. In *The Latin American Program: Ethnic Conflict and Governance in Comparative Perspective*. Washington, DC: Woodrow Wilson International Center for Scholars.

Stinchcombe, Arthur. 1978. *Theoretical Methods in Social History*. New York: Academic Press.

Stephan, A. 1998. "Democratic Opposition and Democratization Theory." *Government and Opposition*, 32(4) (Autumn): 657–73.

Stephan, L. 1995. "The Zapatista Army of National Liberation and the National Democratic Convention." *Latin American Perspectives*, 87(22) (Fall): 88–99.

Stephens, John D. 1993. "Capitalist Development and Democracy: Empirical Research on the Social Origins of Democracy," pp. 409–47. In *The Idea of Democracy*, edited by D. Coop, J. Hampton, and J. Roemer. Cambridge: Cambridge University Press.

Swidler, Ann. 1973. "The Concept of Rationality in the Work of Max Weber." *Sociological Inquiry*, 43: 35–42.

Szelenyi, S., I. Szelenyi, and W. Poster. 1996. "Interests and Symbols in Post-Communist Political Culture: The Case of Hungary." *American Sociological Review*, 61 (June): 466–77.

"Taiwanese General Social Change Survey." 1992. Sponsored by the National Science Council, Republic of China. Conducted by the Sun Yat-Sen Institute of Social Sciences and Philosophy of Academica Sinica, Taipei, Taiwan, and directed by Drs. Chium Hei-Yuan, Ying-hwa, and Chang.

Tagle, Silva. 1998. "Incorporate the Vote of Mexican Residents in the US Demand Academics, PRD and PAN Members." *Excelsior* (November 30).

Tate, C. Neal. 1987. "Judicial Institutions in Cross-national Perspective: Toward Integrating Courts into the Comparative Study of Politics." In *Comparative Judicial Systems*. London: Butterworth.

Tate, C. Neal. 1993. "Courts and Crisis Regimes: A Theory Sketch with Asian Case Studies." *Political Research Quarterly* (formerly *Western Political Q.*), 46: 311.

Tate, C. Neal and Stacia L. Haynie. 1993. "Authoritarianism and the Function of Courts: A Time Series Analysis of the Philippine Supreme Court, 1961–1987." *Law & Society Review*, 27(4).

Therborn, Goran. 1977. "The Rule of Capital and the Rise of Democracy." *New Left Review*, 103: 3–41.

Therborn, G. 1979. "The Travail of Latin American Democracy." *New Left Review*, 113–14 (January–April).

Therborn, G. 1990. "Suffrage and the Rise of Political Modernity: A Global Perspective on Trajectories and Contexts." Paper presented at UCLA Center for Social Theory and Comparative History Colloquial Series.

Tocqueville, Alexis de. 1976. *Democracy in America*. Vols. 1 and 2. New York: Knopf.

Toharia, Jose Juan. 1974. "The Spanish Judiciary: A Sociological Study: Justice in a Civil Law Country Undergoing Social Change under an Authoritarian Regime." Ph.D. dissertation, Yale University.

Townsend, William Cameron. 1952. *Lázaro Cárdenas, Mexican Democrat*. Ann Arbor, MI: George Wahr.

Trieber, Hubert. 1981. "'Elective Affinities' between Weber's Sociology of Religion and Sociology of Law," *Theory and Society*, 11: 809–56.

Trubek, David. 1972. "Max Weber on Law and the Rise of Capitalism." *Wisconsin Law Review*, 3: 720–53.

Trubek, David. 1985. "Reconstructing Max Weber's Sociology of Law." *Stanford Law Review*, 37: 919–36.

Trubek, David. 1986. "Max Weber's Tragic Modernism and the Study of Law in Society." *Law & Society Review*, 20(4): 573–98.

Turner, Bryan S. 1986. *Citizenship and Capitalism: The Debate over Reformism*. London: Allen & Unwin.

"The Two Faces of Dual Nationality: America Should Not Accept Mexico's New Law Allowing Dual Citizenship." 1998. *Insight on the News*, 14(22) (June 15): 48.

Ugalde, Luis Carlos. 1999. "Executive-Legislative Relations in Mexico: The Case of Legislative Oversight of Public Expenditures." Ph.D. dissertation, Columbia University.

"Una casa de cristal." 1976. *Triunfo* (October 30), 10.

Underwood, Kenneth Dale. 1998. "The Mexican Congress and Democratization in Mexico." Ph.D. dissertation, Texas A&M University-Kingsville.

Urzua, Carlos M. 1997. "How to Provoke an Economic Crisis: The Mexican Way," pp. 34–52. In *Mexico: Assessing Neo-Liberal Reform*. London: Institute of Latin American Studies.

Valenzuela, Samuel J. 1992. "Democratic Consolidation in Post-Transitional Settings: Notion, Process, and Facilitating Conditions," pp. 57–104. In *Issues in Democratic Consolidation: The New South American Democracies in Comparative Perspective*, edited by Scott Mainwaring, Guillermo D'Donnell, and J. Samuel Valenzuela. Notre Dame: University of Notre Dame Press.

Verner, Joel G. 1984. "The Independence of Supreme Courts in Latin America: A Review of the Literature." *Journal of Latin American Studies*, 16: 463.

Victorio, R. 1999. "The Creation of New Municipalities in Chiapas: A Social, Economic and National Security Strategy." *Excelsior* (April 4).

Von Lazar, Arpad. 1971. *Latin American Politics*. Boston: Allyn and Bacon.

Weber, Max. 1978. *Economy and Society*. Vols. I and II. Berkeley: University of California Press.

Weinert, Richard S. 1977. "Introduction." In *Authoritarianism in Mexico*, edited by J.L. Reyna, and R.S. Weinert. Philadelphia: Institute for the Study of Human Issues.

Wilkie, James, ed. 1990. *Statistical Abstract of Latin America*. Los Angeles: University of California Press.

Wilkie, James, ed. 1995. *Statistical Abstract of Latin America*. Los Angeles: UCLA Latin American Center.

Woldenburg, Jose. 1997. "The Future of the Mexican Left," pp. 36–52. In *Mexico: Assessing Neo-Liberal Reform*. London: Institute of Latin American Studies.

Wolfe, C. 1986. *The Rise of Modern Judicial Review: From Constitutional Interpretation to Judge-Made Law*. New York: Basic Books.

Yates, Lamartine P. 1981. *Mexico's Agricultural Dilemma*. Tucson: University of Arizona Press.

Zabludovsky, Gina Kuper. 1984. "Racionalidad formal y material: Max Weber y el pensamiento neoconservador." *Revista Mexicana de Ciencias Sociales y Politicas*, 118: 49–68.

Zabludovsky, Gina Kuper. 1986. "Max Weber y La Dominacion Patrimonial en America Latina." *Revista Mexicana de Ciencias Politicas y Sociales*, 124: 75–95.

Zebadua, E. 1998. "Vote Abroad." [Voto en el extranjero]. *La Jornada* (November 21).

Index

About the Author

SARA SCHATZ is an Assistant Professor of sociology at the University of Florida.

ISBN 0-275-96666-6

9 780275 966669

HARDCOVER BAR CODE